God Talk

and Other
Incoherent Religious Delusions

God Talk

and Other
Incoherent Religious Delusions

For Lee

All the Best, —

❖

Rodney Sheffer

L. Rodney Sheffer

Library of Congress Control Number: 2010904658
ISBN: Hardcover   978-1-4500-9779-6
                  Softcover   978-1-4500-9778-9
                  Ebook   978-1-4500-7550-3

This book was printed in the United States of America.

To order additional copies of this book, contact:
Xlibris Corporation
1-888-795-4274
www.Xlibris.com
Orders@Xlibris.com
79121

19 Science, Religion and Change 132
20 Some Questions for Christians 136
21 The Fatal Flaw in the Thinking of St. Augustine 144
22 The Evolution of Gods, Violence, and Public Education ..148
23 The Evolution of Moral Values 154
24 The Quest for Certainty and Absolutes 158
25 Archbishop Ussher, Religious Fundamentalism and
   Modern Science 162
26 What is the Bible? 166
27 Biblical Sexual Standards 170
28 Dinosaurs, Christianity, Evolution and Extinction 174
29 The Jesus of the Gospels: History or Myth? 178
30 Rethinking the God Hypothesis in the 21st Century 184
31 Is The Bible the Word of an Omniscient God? 192
32 Jesus of Nazareth: True or False? 194
33 Are Gods and Religion in Our Future? 198
34 Is the Bible Historically Accurate? 202
35 Scientific or Religious Epistemologies? 206
36 A Letter to 21st Century Parents 210
37 Some Thoughts by a Scientist on Faith and
   Religion While Working in My Garden 213

About the Author 293

Contents

Preface 7
Introduction... 9
Acknowledgments... 13

Chapter

1   In the Beginning 16
2   Defining God: Yours And Mine... 26
3   The Bible: A Source of Truth in Our Time? 32
4   On Religious Faith: Its Implications,
    Risks and Consequences.. 38
5   Why Science Works and Why Religion Fails 46
6   The King, The Priest and We The People 50
7   Gods, Power and the Origin of Religions 54
8   The Ten Revolutionary Changes That Human Beings Must
    Make to Avoid Possible Extinction in the 21st Century....... 60
9   Ten Criteria For Believing 76
10 Liberty, Freedom, and Justice for All 80
11 Absolutism, Religious Fundamentalism,
    and Our Evolving Culture.. 84
12 Twelve Reasons Why I Reject Christianity.......................... 92
13 Finding Truth in Our Lives 98
14 Getting Up to Speed in the Twenty First Century.............. 104
15 Logic and Theology: A Syllogism and Case Study 112
16 Mr. Townsend, Faith and Truth 118
17 My God Exists!.. 122
18 The Objective and the Subjective:
    Two Domains of Thinking 126

Preface

This book is a collection of essays, thoughts and ideas that were written and collected over a period of more than 30 years in different locations often in response to an event or circumstance in my life that provided the stimulus to put my ideas on the subject to paper. Consequently, there is neither plot nor any kind of continuity to the content from chapter to chapter. The reader is advised, however, that since there is a unifying theme throughout all of the essays, the recurrence of some ideas or expressions is inevitable and unavoidable. Each of the essays stands alone and has its own end point. This can be an advantage for the reader because the book can be read in small segments and be conveniently consumed and "digested" in a piecemeal fashion.

Since all writers are voracious readers, it is inevitable that their reading influences their writing. All writers borrow—either consciously or unconsciously—from other writers. While responsible writers rigorously eschew plagiarism, it is probably impossible for a writer to compose essays or viewpoints on a subject without any of the flavor or substance from other writers. However, everything in this book represents my thought, my philosophy and my world view.

The content of this book leaves no doubt that I am a nonbeliever, I am a non-theist, I am a Freethinker, I am an atheist for all of the right and good reasons. I am a secular, scientific, ethical Humanist. There is no place for irrationality, superstition or magical thinking in my understanding of the universe. My highest priorities are academic honesty and intellectual integrity.

Introduction

In recent years there have been a plethora of superb books written about atheism—and atheistic apologetics—that have raised the level of awareness of millions of people, especially some religious believers. Some of these books were written by scientists: Dr. Richard Dawkins, (a biologist), Dr. Victor J. Stenger and Dr. Taner Edis (physicists), philosophers Dr. Daniel Dennett, Dr. Michael Martin, Dr. Michael Onfray, Dr. Paul Kurtz and Dr. Walter Kaufmann. Others, such as Sam Harris, Christopher Hitchens, and Dan Barker have made major contributions. Interestingly, some excellent books were written by former Roman Catholic priests e.g., Stephen F. Uhl; protestant ministers/pastors, e.g., John W. Loftus who struggled with the absurdities and immanent contradictions of their religious faith until they felt compelled to abandon it all for the purpose of reestablishing their sense of academic honesty and intellectual integrity. Having spent a good share of their life living a lie had become so emotionally traumatic for them that regaining peace of mind and a quiet heart became a higher priority for them than the certitude, constancy and predictability that religious platitudes and dogma could no longer provide.

Even theologians with impressive academic credentials like Bishop John Shelby Spong and Dr. Robert M. Price, have come to grips with the reality that theism is no longer an intellectually defensible idea. Biblical scholars have determined that the Bible is not the record of factual history that the Roman Catholic Church has touted for centuries. Rather, after much rigorous scholarly examination, many have labeled much of the Bible as fiction, fraud, and forgery with plenty of justification. Thus, the veracity of much of the Bible has been severely compromised in the minds of educated people.

Former Protestant fundamentalist preachers such as Lee Salisbury heads a substantial and growing list of people who found that the cognitive dissonance in the Christian scheme of things created so much internal conflict that they felt compelled to jettison the bogus baggage that had been dragging them down for so long.

Educated people are less and less inclined to accept mythology as history. While a sacred narrative may be an important part of people's lives, any such story that helps to define who we are must, of necessity, be consistent with and in accord with a modern, scientific knowledge base. Ancient and archaic stories that deny and defy the known laws of the universe do not carry the credibility necessary for educated people who more and more employ critical thinking and higher order thinking skills to successfully navigate the rocky rapids in the river of life. People with a modicum of intellectual sophistication recognize that assessing and evaluating information that comes to them from a wide variety of sources requires an approach to problem solving that begins with a healthy measure of skepticism about the claims and assertions that bombard them daily. Credulousness when faced with the modern techniques of persuasion leaves one very vulnerable to being exploited and manipulated by unscrupulous and unprincipled people from both the secular and the ecclesiastical realms. Americans who value freedom of expression have to be able to recognize and defend themselves from the Elmer Gantrys of the world. When warm fuzzy falsehoods that may feel good are dropped on us, we have to be able to recognize them for the lies they are and treat them appropriately. Mucking around in the trash bin of the history of obsolete ideas to find salvation or direction for our lives will not and cannot serve our best interests.

Today we recognize that all gods, whether one believes in one or many, are the product of fertile, but unsophisticated human imaginations. Gods were invented by the more imaginative people in the Neolithic tribe—usually the priests or the ruling class—to suit their perceived needs as they sought to maintain their dominion over the ignorant and illiterate masses. Preying on the ignorant and gullible masses who needed to explain the contingencies and vicissitudes in their lives has always been an effective tool for controlling and manipulating people. Unfortunately, it still is.

No one has been able to demonstrate that beseeching or imploring one god has ever been more efficacious than another, whether Semitic, Nordic, Greek, Polynesian or any other. Neolithic humans, trying desperately to explain the natural phenomena in their environment, created explanatory models in animal and human forms (sometimes even chimeras), and we call them "gods." Now we are seeing what appears to be a natural evolutionary trend from polytheism/pantheism to monotheism, and in our time to post theism, as more and more people demand a modern, scientific explanation to understand the natural phenomena in their lives. Deities of any kind are no longer a part of the thinking of adequately educated people because deities/gods can no longer be intellectually justified. All mythologies must be understood and explained as the fiction they are no matter how comfortable they might feel or how convenient they might be. Fideism and theology are historical fossils and a cultural dead end. Divesting ourselves of the superstition, magical thinking, and anthropomorphic projections of the monotheistic religions is now our most important cultural imperative. It can only be accomplished with appropriate education. We need to start now!

Acknowledgments

I am deeply indebted to my multitalented wife Carol, for her invaluable help in the production of this book. As a one-time career teacher of English, creative writing, humanities, publications, and a magazine editor she is eminently qualified to be my advisor, critic and editor. I just got lucky I guess.

Most of her suggestions have been incorporated into the text of this book, but I stubbornly refused to take her advice on some points. Consequently, I am solely responsible for all errors of either content or style.

We can measure the degree of validation or authentication of our lives by the level of our education. Truly educated people do not require an external source for that validation or authentication—they create their own. Uneducated, or inadequately educated people, seek that validation from a god. The god hypothesis is meaningless for an adequately educated person.

—L. Rodney Sheffer

~~~~~~~~~~~~~~~~~~~

A first class liberal arts education will allow you to live comfortably with doubt, irony, ambiguity, uncertainty and paradox. If you need absolute certainty you can invent your own infallible god.

—L. Rodney Sheffer

In the Beginning

Random chance mutations and other factors that influence the spontaneous changes acting independently on a population of primates that had become reproductively isolated from others of its kind provided the evolutionary event that caused the genetic split that separated our hominid ancestor from the pongid ancestor. This led to the evolutionary split between proto humans and chimpanzees circa five million years ago, according to the best evidence available at this time. In spite of this long period of time separating these two closely related species from their common ancestor, it has been determined that chimpanzees and humans have about 99 percent of their genes in common. In this speciation event one of the paired chromosomes of the hominid line experienced a permanent separation of one pair of chromosomes into two pair. This accounts for the fact that while chimpanzees have 22 pairs of chromosomes per cell, humans have 23 pairs. The diploid number for chimpanzees is 44, and for humans it is 46.

This is the tentative and provisional conclusion that physical anthropologists and biologists have made based on the available evidence from the fossil record and our knowledge of molecular genetics and cytology. Since that genetic split occurred, the evolution of the hominid branch of the primate lineage has produced a plethora of species, all but one of which has become extinct. The only hominid to survive the selection pressures of the environment is human beings—Homo sapiens sapiens. Homo sapiens means Man-the-Wise. There is a strong argument that posits that the scientific binomial is a misnomer.

Since the population that gave rise to the lineage that produced humans spread and became adapted to local conditions, further mutations resulted in genetic variation within local populations of humans. This accounts for the different races of inter-fertile humans. While humans spread over great land masses into isolated populations, there apparently has not been enough time for separate populations of humans to be reproductively isolated to result in two or more "human" species. Today, all humans in spite of some superficial differences, are reproductively of a single species.

Succeeding generations of a number of species showed an increase in brain size over the course of time. Cranial and cerebral sizes reached their present size and development somewhere between 150 million and 200 million years ago. There has been no discernible increase in average skull or cerebral size in this window of time. The increase in size of the human skull at birth had to be matched by the increase in size of the human female pelvic structure. Some women today might argue that their pelvic width was not big enough or wide enough to accommodate the passage of their big-brained fetus. Indeed, the birth of a human baby is still a life threatening event for the mother. So much for the claim that humans are the product of intelligent design. It boggles the mind how any woman who had ever given birth to a full term fetus would endorse the idea that she was designed by an intelligent male deity.

With an increase in brain size, especially the prefrontal lobe, came the possibility of greater brain complexity. This has resulted in a brain that has a level of complexity that makes human intelligence possible.

The companion feature of human intelligence is the phenomenon we call consciousness. Consciousness is the awareness of self. Consciousness allows us to reflect on the past and extrapolate to the future. Consciousness is the recognition that we humans have a finite time for our lives like every other living thing on our planet. It is the understanding that when we die there is absolute annihilation and total oblivion. This hard cold fact of our existence is without doubt the most terrifying reality of our existence for most people. It is so terrifying that primitive imaginations have created many means to try to come to grips with this reality. Believing that we can somehow survive the death of our bodies, which we recognize is inevitable, is what people want more than anything else in their entire lives. If someone didn't promise us that there was a way or means to survive the death of our body most of us would probably invent our own way, albeit it would be irrational and illogical, based on our present knowledge base. However, that hasn't stopped many people from creating a comfortable illusion that would ameliorate the terror of impending death.

Reestablishing our relationship with our parents, family members and others we love after death is the highest priority in most people's lives in spite of the fact that there is no way to know that this is even possible.

Death denial seems to be a near universal human behavioral trait. All human societies have created a kind of spiritual existence to enable their fantasy of life after death. Consciousness, it seems, is a double-edged sword. We need to be aware, however, that the comfortable ideas we create or borrow from others are no guarantee of truth.

For nearly all of human history we could only draw on the collective knowledge base of our tribe. With a seemingly inborn fear of "other" called xenophobia, intertribal exchange of knowledge was slow and precarious. Hence, intellectual hybrid vigor and an expanding knowledge base was achieved sporadically and piecemeal. There were no libraries or universities.

The human brain was now capable of asking questions. At the same time we demanded answers and explanations as we sought to master and exploit our environment to our advantage.

In the absence of any scientifically based knowledge, there would naturally be an attempt to explain the natural phenomena with which early humans had to contend. Thunderstorms and tornadoes seemed to come out of nowhere. Earthquakes and tsunamis arrived without warning. Thunder and lightning and rain happened irregularly, but no one knew why. In middle and high latitudes the seasons came regularly, but no one knew why. With the phenomenon of consciousness, people were able to ask pointed questions about "why" and "how." What they needed and wanted were reliable answers.

Children asked their parents their why and how questions. Sometimes the parents did not have answers to their questions, so they sought answers from the local "authority figures." These were the tribal chief, or king, or prince, or others of the ruling class. The other "authority figures" in the tribe were the shamans, medicine men, or the priests who were always in collusion with the chief or king. They were the "authority figures" of the tribe. They were authoritarian as well as authoritative. They had to be to maintain their position of dominance and hegemony. They could never appear to be without an answer because if they appeared to be clueless this would diminish their image of authenticity and their hold on their position of authority. If they did not have a ready answer for the restless masses, they could make one up on the spot. This was the origin of revealed truth. If they were questioned about the veracity of their answer, they could invoke divine sanction of an extant god, or they could invent gods as needed. In any event, the masses could accept the "revealed truths" of the ruling hierarchy or go elsewhere. Rulers with divine sanction and a need to maintain their tenuous position of authority did not take kindly to dissent or even debate. To dissent or even question authoritarian dictates was an invitation for severe punishment—often death for sedition, rebellion, or blasphemy. Such has always been the response of totalitarians to challenges to their authority—real or imagined. Power went to and was held by those who could seize the power. They held this power until they died, or it was taken from them.

In the absence of any science and explanatory theories or data, and faced with a plethora of natural phenomena that they could not explain, local authority figures felt a need for external validation on which they could depend to answer pointed questions from the restless, inquiring masses. The fertile imaginations of the ruling class created gods as explanatory paradigms. Whenever a natural phenomenon defied explanation, members of the ruling class could invoke an old, well-known deity or, if needs be, create a new god. Manipulating the masses with wit and guile became a fine art. Thus, politics and religion became a part of everyday life as social dynamics answered the demands of those in power. With a burgeoning pantheon of gods it was inevitable that there evolved a hierarchy of gods. There were lesser gods, middling gods, and greater gods. Predictably perhaps, at least in many cultures, there would emerge in the evolution of deities, a highest or chief god who ruled over all others.

When different cultures, each with many gods, came in contact, it became clear that there were many gods that were in common with those of other cultures, albeit with different names. With hundreds of gods in daily life with nearly everyone, there were apparently no real conflicts among the believers over which held dominion over others. With so many gods with different levels of power and authority, people could invoke one god or many as suited their perceived needs.

Gods were an explanatory paradigm that people could invoke to explain whatever it was that they did not understand. In all of human history nothing much changed in this regard until some people thought that they had a better way when they instituted a method of observation, analysis, interpretation and evaluation to arrive at truths that were dependable and reliable. This new paradigm rejected revealed truth from authority figures and provided a means of truth telling about natural phenomena to everyone. We call this new paradigm science.

Old ways persist, however, as cultural memes that become deeply imbedded as the neural pathways of the brain become indelibly impressed and nearly impossible to erase or abandon. Even in the light of new knowledge that contradicts extant knowledge people are loathe to adopt new ideas that represent change in either values or the physical and factual in their lives. Proposing change of almost any kind makes most people nervous and apprehensive. They can suffer great angst when confronted by the prospect of change of almost any kind. Therefore, they view most changes as threatening and disruptive in their lives. Those who are most likely to behave in this manner we call "Conservatives." Those who are least likely to be anxious about change—those who are most likely to be accepting of diversity, tolerant of variation, paradox, ambiguity and uncertainty are the innovators, the explorers and inventors of new ways we call "Liberals." Conservatives are not agents of reform even when reforms are necessary. Conservatives are very much addicted to the status quo, while Liberals are those who dare to experiment and explore new ideas and new ways. In so doing they acquire the label of "Progressives." Cultural advance is always driven by liberal, progressive personalities. It was the Liberals who lifted human kind out of our troglodyte early existence. It was the Liberals who had to drag the Conservatives out of their caves, kicking and screaming, so that we could rise to the next higher level of civilization. Nothing has changed in this regard in all of human history. One could easily hypothesize that the Liberals have evolved into a more advanced kind of human while the Conservatives lagged behind and devolved into Neanderthals, but the compassionate Liberals with their social safety nets for all, kept dragging the Conservatives along and kept them in the gene pool long enough to save them from extinction. Alas, some altruistic behaviors proved to be maladaptive and the gene pool has been degraded. Conservative genes persist among us like genetic detritus that holds us back evolutionarily from evolving into Homo intelligenticus. Truly, evolution has neither a plan, nor direction, nor goal. Conservatives are living proof that some humans persist in the gene pool as defective, recessive genomes.

As chronically conservative paradigms, religions have always been addicted to the status quo. In rapidly evolving cultures and societies, religions have invariably found themselves being left behind in antiquated obsolescence that fails to adapt to the inevitable changing mores and vicissitudes of human existence. Consequently they become archaic and irrelevant in the relentless march toward modernity. The ignorance, superstition and magical thinking that characterized the monotheistic religions many centuries ago is perpetuated and promulgated today by the conservative mind set of the priesthood and secular conservatives. Evolution of any kind is always anathema to conservatives because it represents change.

There is an old adage that says nothing is certain except death and taxes. To this we must add "change." Change is the most inevitable characteristic of the world whether it be the physical changes in the earth's crust, volcanism or the weathering of rocks. The nature of RNA and DNA molecules under the influences of background radiation and other environmental influences results in constant change in all of the genomes of the world. The natural replication of DNA and RNA is remarkably consistent, uniform and accurate, but it is, none the less, imperfect. The result of different kinds of errors in this natural process is just one of the factors that generates the variation in genetic codes that result in the mutations that have assured the continuous and inevitable process of organic evolution. We can't help it and we can't stop it. We can only accept the reality of organic evolution and try to understand it—even use it to our advantage. While some people are seemingly locked onto the ancient idea that their favorite deity is responsible for all that is or will be, modern science has rendered this archaic idea as null and void and totally without cognitive merit. Some people have adjusted to and adopted this modern explanation of reality and some persist in their obstinate, perverse ignorance as the world continues to evolve apace in spite of them.

The failure to adopt and adapt to new knowledge is a part of the definition of stupidity. While no one is either exempt or immune from behaving stupidly on occasion, some people seem to be chronically prone to error. Education is, in part, an attempt by society to help people minimize their proclivity to behaving stupidly. Some people seem to profit greatly from this process and some people seem to resist all attempts for intellectual growth. Some people even remove themselves from the gene pool out of ignorance or stupidity or both.

In the Darwinian struggle for existence in the 21st century those people best equipped with the most modern scientific knowledge base will prove to be the most competitive, and those with an archaic, theological/ Biblical explication of natural phenomena are quite prone to becoming extinct. The question before us now is: Will the necessary evolutionary changes in the human genome take place in time before we destroy our planet, our culture and our continued existence, or will we fail to direct our own evolution at a rate that will allow us to avoid the destiny of the dinosaurs?

Preordained external authority strongly suggests that people are incapable of governing themselves. This is the defense or justification of the divine right of kings and the sacred authority of the priesthood, (Those who claim to have knowledge or direct access to divine authority.) Such a rationale is a direct contradiction of the idea of democratic governance and is the mainstay of those who pathologically seek dominion over others. The more the populace becomes educated, the more civilized they become, and the more capable they become of democratic governance. It then follows that when people become more educated, they have less need for external authority. Gods are for the uneducated and the uncivilized. Gods are needed by the ignorant and the barbaric to provide both prescriptions and proscriptions for their lives. Can people claim to be educated and civilized if they endorse and support the external authority of kings or gods?

Whenever we read the obscene stories, the voluptuous debaucheries, the cruel and tortuous executions, the unending vindictiveness, with which more than half of the Bible is filled, it would be more consistent that we call it the word of a demon than the word of God. It is a history of wickedness that has served to corrupt and brutalize.

—Thomas Paine, *The Age of Reason,* 1792.

~~~~~~~~~~~~~~~~~~

Question with boldness even the existence of God; because if there be one, he must approve the homage of reason rather than that of blindfolded fear.

—Thomas Jefferson

Defining God: Yours And Mine

One day, late in my career as a biology teacher, we had finished our lesson for the day on organic evolution, and there were a few minutes left in the hour. A student asked me if I believed in god. I replied that the question was fair and well received, but that the question was asked at the wrong time and place as this was a science class that dealt with secular subjects only, in a secular institution, supported by a secular state and secular nation. I also made the point that science addresses itself only to our questions about natural phenomena, and has nothing whatever to say about theological, extra-natural, or supernatural subjects.

If she were to ask me off campus if I believed in a god I would first have to ask, "Which one?" because the word "god" could be understood only in a generic context. People have created literally thousands of gods, and therefore the idea of "god" could mean disparate things to many people. In the approximately 150,000 year history of human beings, people have always created their own gods from their own experience and to suit their own purpose whether for their perceived needs or to control others.

I would have asked her, "Specifically, which god are you asking about? If she had said, "The Christian God", I would have replied that I was still at something of a loss for an answer because I did not know what she meant by "god." I would have explained that I had asked maybe a thousand people, both professional and lay people, to define what they meant by "god," and that I had received an equal number of definitions. One young mother had told me that she defined "god" as, "the space between the molecules."

I had read what scores and scores of theologians and philosophers had to say about what or who god was or is, and they all had different opinions, and they all thought they were right and that the others were wrong. Even the early Catholic Church was rent asunder because different factions defined their god in different terms. Now, we can only wonder how many different concepts of "god" there are among 2500 denominations of Protestants.

Some Christian theologians had been accused and convicted of heresy because their ideas about "god" were different from some others. I knew that this had been going on for more than twenty centuries, and there was still no resolution to the differences of opinion, even from those who allegedly knew the most about the subject. The likelihood that I understood "god" in the same context as my student was so remote that if she were asking if I believed in the same idea of god as she did, the answer would statistically have to be "Probably not." This begs the question: "After more than two millennia, are we any closer to having a clearer and more universal understanding of who or what 'god' is?

If she was asking if I believed in an anthropomorphic, paternalistic, patriarchal, personal, creator god (a kind of cosmic designer) who chronically meddled in the lives of people, (a kind of cosmic cop); or a kind of god who meted out rewards and punishments, condemning some people to eternal damnation in a fiery hell for disobedience or unbelief (a kind of cosmic judge) I would have to say, "Surely, you jest."

If she were asking if I believed in a god who blessed some people with remarkable talents while denying them to others, or played favorites by designating some people as his "Chosen People," or made countless egregious errors while creating millions of babies born with horrifying genetic or congenital defects, I would have said, "Not on your life."

If she were asking if I believed in a god who played a role in the generation of natural phenomena (earthquakes, volcanism, tsunamis, tornadoes, hurricanes) without warning people, or who played dice with the universe; or otherwise "watches over us", then all this is nothing more than worship of an idealized form of ourselves. Such a world view is not only elementary and primitive, it is intellectually unsophisticated and indefensible in light of a more modern understanding of natural phenomena. I would have to say, "You've got to be kidding me—please don't insult my intelligence!"

If the most authoritative god believers couldn't agree about what or who "god" was or is, what different believers believed really depended on who they had been listening to; even then there was a lot of disagreement. Christians, Jews, and Muslims all believe that there is only one God, but they have profound differences in what they believe is true about their God. The differences are so great that they have been killing each other over their different beliefs for centuries, and it is still going on. Christians even kill other Christians over their differences. (See Ireland and Yugoslavia.) The same is true for Muslims (see Sunni's and Shia) even though all of them preach the "Golden Rule," forgiveness, charity, tolerance, and "love one another." It seems as though, in spite of all of the rhetoric, the message has been lost, or the message has made little impression on the believers, or that their omniscient and omnipotent God has been either unwilling, incapable or indifferent about doing anything about it.

It seems as though there is an enormous amount of confusion about a subject that should be universally simple, direct and consistent, especially among believers. Such is not the case, and resolution does not appear to be forthcoming.

Some of my Christian friends have suggested that I, like they, should love, honor, obey, and worship their Hebrew god who, according to the most learned theologians is unknowable, indescribable, inscrutable, ineffable, and completely incomprehensible. If we cannot find consensus among theologians as to what or who "God" is, then we cannot escape the idea that those who engage in "God talk" really don't know what they are talking about. We are left hopelessly adrift without a rudder in a stormy sea of semantic obfuscation and blinding confusion, falling headlong into a philosophical black hole. Are these people, then even worthy of our attention? Should we even give consideration to their unverifiable claims and groundless assertions?

I suggested that if we were created in the image of an omniscient "god," and that people have always created their gods in their own image, then such a god must be a lot like us. That being so, then worshiping such a deity would be little more than another form of anthropomorphic idolatry which would be narcissism at its worst. This is not only patently absurd, it is intellectually abhorrent.

So, back to my student's original question—do I believe in God? Almost everyone believes in a god or gods. It depends on how "God" is defined and whose definition is accepted. If we examine and understand our own history, and the history of gods, it is not difficult at all to understand why there is such incredible diversity in our concepts of "God." It just depends on how we define our own idea of "God," or if we accept someone else's concept of "God.

If we accept someone else's concept of "God" on faith, then we are allowing them to do our thinking for us. If people are inadequately educated and/or incapable of thinking for themselves and defining their own god, in their own terms, to their own purposes, then I suppose that is the best they can do. Unthinking people (the ignorant masses) have always believed what thinking people, (the king and the priests) have told them what they should believe and how they should behave. It is not difficult to imagine why so many educated people have rejected that kind of intellectual and emotional manipulation.

If we accept the unsupported and unverifiable claims and assertions of others in the secular world, we will be branded as and known as gullible, credulous fools, and deservedly so. If we accept the unsupported claims and unverifiable assertions as truth from those who claim divine sanction, are we any different from those in a secular context? Is there anyone who thinks we have two brains and a double set of consciousness, one for secular concerns and one for religious concerns? Can we afford to be critical and analytical thinkers on just a part-time basis and abandon our higher thought processes to satisfy our appetite for warm, comfortable emotional trips into wishful thinking and an escape from reality?

Will we educate our children with the highest level of our modern, intellectual knowledge base, or indoctrinate them with ancient, and archaic biases, prejudices and religion-political agendas derived from a tribal mind set to solve the problems they will face in the 21st century?

Do I believe in a god? Certainly not in the context of any of the monotheistic religions which are derived from a pre-modern knowledge base that can best be described as somewhere between Paleolithic conjecture and Bronze Age speculation.

I did believe in a god as a naive child because I was indoctrinated with that idea before I could think critically and evaluate the arguments and the evidence for and against the existence of a god. Like everyone else, I was the product of my environment. Subsequently, however, in the light of a modern, scientific knowledge base, gods of any kind, whether one or many, cannot stand up to critical examination. Gods, like all religions, are grounded in and derived from a profound misunderstanding and misinterpretation of natural phenomena. Gods cannot be reconciled with the realities of the known laws of the universe.

Can I prove that a god or gods do not exist? Of course not. One can never prove a negative, nor is one ever compelled to try to do so. The burden of proof is always on the claimant, and thus far, no one has ever provided a single scintilla of compelling evidence to support the assertion that a god or gods exist.

Nearly everyone understands this. Believing in a god then is a matter of choice—it is a personal option that is exercised according to one's perceived needs and reflects the level of one's understanding of the world and the cosmos in which one lives. If your definition of a god does not agree with mine, that is all right with me. I say you're entitled to your own definition of your god. If my definition does not agree with yours, is that all right with you?

I define god as, "The nature of Nature." This works for me. If it doesn't work for you I will NOT say that you are evil, or immoral, or amoral, or doomed to spend eternity being seared in flames. I will not label you as blasphemous, nor call you a heretic.

If you disagree with my definition of "God," you have just two choices: you can define your god in your own way, in your own terms, to serve your own purpose, or you can let someone else do your thinking for you.

Savage and furious nations, perpetually at war, adore, under diverse names, some God, conformable to their ideas, that is to say, cruel, carnivorous, selfish, bloodthirsty. We find, in all the religions, 'a God of armies,' a 'jealous God,' an 'avenging God,' a 'destroying God,' a 'God,' who is pleased with carnage, and whom his worshippers consider it a duty to serve. Lambs, bulls, children, men, and women, are sacrificed to him. Zealous servants of this barbarous God think themselves obliged even to offer up themselves as a sacrifice to him. Madmen may everywhere be seen, who, after meditating upon their terrible God, imagine that to please him they must inflict on themselves, the most exquisite torments. The gloomy ideas formed of the deity, far from consoling them, have every where disquieted their minds, and prejudiced follies destructive to happiness.

—Baron d'Holbach, Common Sense, 1772.

~~~~~~~~~~~~~~~~~~

The question before the human race is whether the God of Nature shall govern the world by his own laws or whether kings and priests shall rule by fictitious miracles.

—John Adams, in a letter to Thomas Jefferson

The Bible: A Source of Truth in Our Time?

All three of the monotheistic religions (and probably the others as well) are grounded in and derived from a profound misunderstanding and misinterpretation of natural phenomena. This may be a large order to swallow on first examination for some people, but after only a cursory consideration, it is palpably true. The cosmology of the people who constructed and composed both the Bible (Old and New Testaments) and the Koran was and is so blatantly and egregiously wrong that it calls into question the cognitive merits of all of the rest of their ideas about the world in which they lived.

Today, giving assent to the Biblical miracles as divine truths on which we might base or govern our lives is gross foolishness. None of the Biblical "miracles" that defy and deny the known laws of the universe were a factual accounting of reality. None of these "miracles" (in the light of modern science) could have been possible.

We understand that the people who wrote the Biblical narratives were not academic historians (as we understand them), trying to construct an accurate historical record of their time for posterity; they were composing what was supposed to be a sacred story that created "pictures for the mind" intended for the ignorant masses who were in all likelihood more than 98% illiterate. Their intent was to advance a religious agenda among very unsophisticated and uncritical people whose lives were dominated and controlled by the fears and superstitions of their culture in their time. However, (and this is a very big "however") a sacred/holy text would have to be as simple, straight forward, and forthright to all people of all cultures and all times with minimal interpretation; otherwise unconstrained subjectivities and spurious interpretations would create confusions and obfuscation.

A sacred or holy text cannot contain untruths if it is to be credible and of any value. Today, in our culture, the literalist/fundamentalist interpretation of an ancient and archaic text that was composed in total ignorance of all that humanity has learned in the last 2000 years, even the last 150 years, is so badly out of date and so hopelessly irrelevant on so many issues, that trying to create a universal understanding that would be acceptable to all is doomed to failure. Consequently, the Bible should be shelved as a grossly obsolete cultural artifact from an ancient, primitive culture that cannot in any sense be regarded as a relevant resource for life governance in the 21st century. Any sacred text from which we are to derive guidance for our lives must evolve apace with our evolving culture; otherwise it will inevitably be relegated to the dustbin of history as obsolete, as the Bible is today for us.

The assertion by some people that their Bible is the word of their omniscient and omnipotent god of choice, either directly or by divine guidance, is probably the most absurd and intellectually indefensible statement in the history of Western Civilization. The Bible is riddled through and through with hundreds of inconsistencies, contradictions, factual errors, anachronisms, obvious interpolations, editing errors, copyist errors and tribal politics that make such a claim ludicrous in the extreme. The scores of metaphors, allegories, symbolism, and literary license that are either poorly or completely misunderstood by people of our time make a meaningful interpretation a very high-risk affair. As Bishop John Shelby Spong wrote, the adult Bible study groups found in most Protestant churches amount to nothing more than ". . . a pooling of ignorance." These groups who expect to enlighten each other by their brand of amateur scholarship achieve nothing more than confabulation that results in nothing more than a confidence born of communal confusion.

If the Bible is not the word of an omniscient and omnipotent god, then it must be the word of mostly men from a culture that is so alien to ours, and our culture would be so incomprehensible to them, that there is no possible way that their ideas about morals and ethics could be useful or applicable to us. Any ethical or moral code for us in the 21st century must be derived by us from our cumulative knowledge base and our experience. Any attempt to rely on such a code of behavior from such an alien culture cannot serve our collective best interests.

One of the definitions of stupidity is: The failure to acknowledge or the failure to adopt and adapt to new knowledge. Abandonment or rejection of obsolete ideas that have been superseded by new knowledge that has advanced our culture has been the hallmark of civilization for all human history. Some obsolete ideas seem to perish and pass into oblivion easily and completely. Other obsolete or irrelevant ideas seem to persist as cultural memes in spite of the fact that they no longer have cognitive merit among better educated people. As this is inarguably true, we are given to ask why this is so. After all, a demonstrably bad idea or an idea that no longer serves our long-term interests should seem destined for the trash heap of history. The answer seems to be that an idea, in spite of its lack of merit, will persist in our culture if it in any way provides a level of comfort or solace by retaining it. Hence, ideas of the past, even if they are now deemed obsolete or even absurd in the light of our modern, scientific knowledge base, will find refuge among ignorant, credulous people whose comfort requirements will always trump logic, reason, and higher order thinking skills. Some people still don't understand that education should be our highest priority in the 21st century if we are to be competitive in the world market place of modern ideas.

We are constantly bombarded with God talk from the self-appointed and self-authenticating messengers of "The Truth." They never offer any kind of evidence to support their assertions because none exists, but that doesn't seem to bother them one bit. They never offer any external corroboration for their claims. None of their claims of truth are falsifiable, i.e., their assertions cannot be either proven or disproven. Furthermore, they say they do not need evidence to support their assertions because they have their faith that what they were told by others is true because it is the inspired word of their God. This groundless assertion is worth examining if only to expose it for its lack of cognitive merit.

Yahweh, the god of Abraham, the god of the Jews, and the Christians is alleged to be omniscient, omnipotent, omnibenevolent and omnipresent by the believers. If that were true, then their holy books alleged to be the divinely inspired word of a "Perfect Divine Being" could not possibly be in error. The highest levels of Biblical scholarship, however, show clearly and inarguably that this is not true. In the light of modern scholarship, such claims are prevarications.

The Bible, written by many unknown authors over a period of many centuries has been labeled by some competent scholars as fiction, fraud, forgery and fantasy. This mishmash of tribal jealousies, religio-political agendas and astrological superstitions can hardly be regarded as the word of an omniscient, perfect god. What we can understand about the Old Testament is that it was written by Hebrew priests and hireling scribes as a religious myth to lend strength to their ambitions as authoritarian "prophets" whose appetite for dominion over the masses was rarely satisfied. The ancient Hebrews who didn't even have their own alphabet until somewhere between 1000 and 800 years B.C.E. were thousands of years behind surrounding and competing societies in the development and recording of their culture. Today, the assertion that the Bible is the Word of God is probably the most intellectually indefensible statement in the history of Western Civilization. In spite of this, the perpetuators and promulgators of this religio/political myth that has been touted as factual history, have persisted in exploiting the ignorance and fears of the gullible, credulous masses with deadly effectiveness. Conditioned to be believers from infancy, the huge majority of people continue to be victimized by those who find it lucrative to continue the intellectual travesty and duplicity of religious irrationality.

Indelibly impressed since early childhood, most people are incapable of jettisoning the irrational baggage of their religious indoctrination even when presented with the modern scholarship that renders their archaic beliefs utterly null and void. Comfortably ensconced in an irrational cognitive trap, most people who have been victimized by their religious indoctrination are loathe to abandon the intellectual prison that has been their only emotional "home" for their entire life. Velvet covered shackles are still shackles.

If faith cannot be reconciled with rational thinking, it has to be eliminated as an anachronistic remnant of earlier stages of culture and replaced with science dealing with facts and theories which are intelligible and can be validated.

—Eric Fromm, Man for Himself (1947)

~~~~~~~~~~~~~~~~~~~~

The religious persecution of the ages has been done under what was claimed to be the command of God. I distrust those people who know so well what God wants them to do to their fellows because it always coincides with their own desires.

—Susan B. Anthony (1820-1906)

On Religious Faith:
Its Implications, Risks and Consequences.

When confronted with the charge that their religious allegations of truth have no evidentiary support and cannot be verified, I invariably hear people say, "We don't need evidence or verification because our beliefs are based on our "faith." This raises some questions:

- What is faith, and what are its implications?
- Can faith-based beliefs serve our best interests?
- What are the historical consequences of faith-based beliefs?
- Are there inherent hazards in faith-based beliefs?
- Are faith-based beliefs consistent with higher order thinking skills, and a modern knowledge base?
- Who makes an advantage or profit from the promulgation of claims and assertions based on faith? Of necessity, we must address these questions.

How can we characterize or define or understand and explain "faith?" Webster's New World College Dictionary, Fourth Ed., defines "faith" as, "Unquestioning belief without proof or evidence." In addition to the dictionary there are other ways to accurately describe or characterize what people understand as "faith."

In our culture, being a "person of faith" carries with it an unspoken, but understood, label of being "good." "People of faith" carry a self-imposed position of superiority over those who are not "people of faith." Some "people of faith" regard themselves as "the chosen ones." Diligent scholars who think that all ideas are subject to scrutiny, analysis and evaluation, should do the same for the idea of "faith" being "good," or in some way, desirable.

In a court of law, or the scientific enterprise, or virtually any everyday discourse among educated people, claims or assertions that cannot be supported by compelling evidence and verification would be regarded as specious at best. Information from any single source without external corroboration can be dismissed as propaganda. Hence, claims or assertions that are unsupported by verifiable evidence and external corroboration are cognitively worthless. Clearly, placing credibility in any such unsupported claims or assertions would put people in extreme intellectual jeopardy. At the same time they would be vulnerable to all kinds of mischief and mayhem from ambitious or unprincipled people.

Saul of Tarsus, also known as Saint Paul, was a Hellenized Jew who lived in the first century of the Common Era. He was thoroughly familiar with the pagan mystery religions so common in the area bounded by the eastern Mediterranean Sea. His beliefs about a Christ figure were not based on any evidence that he could produce or verify, rather his beliefs were based on dreams, visions, and what he wanted to be true. In his Biblical letter to the Hebrews, (11:1) he allegedly wrote, "Now faith is the assurance of things hoped for, the conviction of things not seen." This can be paraphrased as: Faith is a guarantee of the propositions that you want to be true, and the belief, as real, in those things that have not been witnessed. Any judge in a court of law, or a reputable scientist, would condemn and reject any such kind of declaration describing truth as being without support or justification, and consequently without merit. Hence, giving assent to a proposition without supporting evidence and verification is giving assent because that is what one wants, not because it is what is intellectually honest and defensible. Consequently, this kind of "truth by faith" opens the door for a host of intellectual errors.

Historically, the most disastrous kinds of intellectual errors are public policies that have been derived as faith-based initiatives, for example: The Crusades, The Spanish Inquisition, and The Holocaust. Beliefs based on emotion and faith are those that most often lead to dreadful consequences. Faith-based initiatives are the sole support of extremism and absolutism that ultimately cascade into persecution and violence. Invariably these faith-based initiatives have resulted in the death and mutilation of millions of people. Reflective thought and critical thinking based on reason, logic and verifiable evidence has been subordinated to subjective, faith-based ideologies. Faith-based thinking is so prone to gross error that the result, more often than not, is tragic. It seems as though people have evolved with a subjective, analog brain trying to make sense out of an objective, digital world. In the long distant past our analog brains have been evolutionarily adaptive for our survival as a species. Today, however, in our modern, scientific, technologically oriented society, our culture demands an objective, rational approach to problem solving for our survival.

When people accept an idea or policy as truth without any confirming or corroborating evidence, we call this a "Leap of Faith." Soren Kierkegaard, the Danish philosopher, accepted on faith the virgin birth of Jesus as a historical fact. He wrote, "Religious faith is a pure leap of will uncontaminated by reason or empirical knowledge." However, beliefs based on faith that are contradictory to the laws of the universe are wrong regardless of the source of their inspiration or who advocates them. John Locke, the English philosopher, wrote, "One unerring mark of the love of truth is not entertaining any proposition with greater assurance than the proofs it is built upon will earn it." Truth by faith means "anything goes." Truth by faith corrupts honest inquiry and skews the data of legitimate research. Intelligent, educated people practice restraint and reflective thinking before giving tentative and provisional assent to the claims and assertions of others. In the absence of compelling evidence and verification, faith easily becomes unwarranted conviction in unjustified assertions. For example: the Bible was inspired by a deity, we will be reunited with our loved ones after we die, the Creator of the universe hears our prayers, or we can conquer pathogens in our body by petitionary prayer.

While the literature of faith is a collection of subjective, mystical, mythological, allegorical narratives that some use to explain themselves whether they are well reasoned or not, faith also absolves people from taking responsibility for themselves and results in conviction without thought. We need to consider, however, that we protect ourselves with reason, logic and critical thinking skills—not with magic, faith or superstition.

Any religion based on faith is a kind of philosophical rigidity that retards progressive development of human culture. Christians, Jews and Muslims are frozen in the tracks of their lesser understanding, wallowing in faith-based fictions and absurd semantic seductions. Creativity is stifled when institutions demand or encourage people to accept on faith their dogmatically revealed religions.

Subjective certitudes, like faith, can be used to sanction any kind of fanaticism or atrocity. People who establish truth in their lives based on faith can believe in anything no matter how illogical or irrational or absurd. They can also justify any behavior including murder and genocide. While not demanding compelling evidence, nor reproducibility, nor confirmation of any kind, faith is the original "no brainer."

Religious faith is a flimsy veil of alleged truths, wishful thinking and warm fuzzy illusions that has entrapped the ignorant, the naive and the credulous. Escaping the trap can only be accomplished with education—not more indoctrination. Given the ability of the human brain to think rationally, the blind faith of revealed religions is the negation of our humanity and is therefore immoral.

If we can explain our relationship with nature in naturalistic terms to our intellectual satisfaction, explaining it in an extra-natural (supernatural) context based on faith is not only unnecessary, it is unwarranted and dangerous. Religious faith tries to turn thought into the process of finding a simplistic, transcendent solution for the complex issue of trying to understand and explain natural phenomena. Of course, this has never worked, but in our scientific, technological culture it is futile, hopeless and dangerous.

If faith is acting on a nobler hypothesis, the nobler hypothesis can never contain untestable, unverifiable or unfalsifiable assertions. When faith, wishful thinking and subjective, theological speculations are raised to the level of objective fact, we witness the reality of superstition. With faith one can excuse or evade the necessity of evaluating the evidence. In the realm of religious faith, facts are irrelevant.

Truth by faith is easy when people fail to search for evidence and employ reason to support a claim or assertion. Truth by faith is "The School of Easy Answers."

Absolute faith corrupts as thoroughly as absolute truth. Absolute truth based on faith is a deterrent to all further research and intellectual inquiry. Faith is the mother of all doctrine and dogma which shut the door to all skepticism, new knowledge, critical inquiry and experimentation.

The arguments of religionists more often than not depend on the uncritical acceptance of imprecise analogies. The results are intellectual errors that seriously obstruct our search for truth. Man-made dogmas and doctrines derived from faith along with ornate rituals and powerful emotions do not validate the flimsy ideas and irrational premises of revealed religions.

Religion rejects reason and logic and replaces it with dogma and blind faith, but we should judge claims and assertions by the test of evidence, reason and logic, not by faith or popular acclaim. Both faith and critical thinking are mental paradigms that people use for deriving their decisions and future actions. The roots of faith are in our volatile emotions, and the roots of critical thinking are in our rational intellect. This dichotomy is worthy of our consideration.

Only convictions that are derived from one or more of the human senses can be justified as knowledge. Other convictions deserve to be known only as belief or faith. The tendentious fictions of the Bible, proffered as the "Word of God" by zealous priests apparently do not require much salesmanship to ignorant, credulous people. We need to be very circumspect about what we accept as truth, based on faith, from any source.

A perfect recipe for social disaster consists of equal portions of unbounded passion, conscientious stupidity, total commitment, willful ignorance and blind faith.

Our most pressing problem in America today is that our legislators are intellectually handicapped by the subjective, religious straitjacket of faith that predisposes them to error as they attempt to deal objectively and rationally with the real problems of the world.

In the history of humankind some people have always sought to exploit others for their own personal gain for either power or material wealth. There are several ways this objective has been implemented. Pressure and coercion, threats of death at the point of a sword, and the most insidious and pernicious of all has been the control of people's behavior by controlling their minds. When the King and the Bishop have all of the authority that they claim has divine sanction, they have total, nearly unbeatable power for the control of the restless masses. The tool for this control is and has always been faith-based revealed religion. Faith-based doctrines built on fear, guilt, shame, and sin are powerful strategies for controlling the minds and behavior of people.

In the absence of a healthy level of skepticism toward the claims and assertions of others, regardless of their position of authority, faith-based belief systems are the favorite tool for the oppression, even persecution, of others. The priest and the pastor demand unquestioning acceptance of their "message." The last thing they want from those being indoctrinated is skepticism, rigorous questioning, and higher order thinking skills. Authoritarian, totalitarian systems of governance imposed on people are dependent on the blind acceptance and total obedience of faith-based ideologies. When these absolutist regimes crack and start coming apart at the seams, people start getting all sorts of crazy, aberrant, even revolutionary, ideas such as: freedom of conscience and expression, personal liberty, freedom of association, and the freedom to criticize and question authority figures. Faith-based belief systems are a constant threat to a democratically governed society. The greatest threats to faith-based belief systems have always been skepticism, rigorous inquiry, and an expanding knowledge base.

In the world market place of competing ideas in the 21st century, the most important and critical issue before us is the education of our children who will require a skeptical approach to truth seeking, the highest order critical thinking skills at our command, and a scientific approach to problem solving. We ignore this cultural imperative at our peril.

Those who take refuge behind theological barbed wire fences quite often wish they could have more freedom of thought, but fear the change that the great ocean of scientific truth as they would take a cold bath plunge.

—Luther Burbank

~~~~~~~~~~~~~~~~~~~

My respect for the Abrahamic religions went up in the smoke and choking dust of September 11th. The last vestige of respect for the taboo disappeared as I watched the "Day of Prayer" in Washington Cathedral, where people of mutually incompatible faiths united in homage to the very force that caused the problem in the first place: religion. It is time for people of intellect, as opposed to people of faith, to stand up and say "Enough!" Let our tribute to the dead be a new resolve: to respect people for what they individually think, rather than respect groups for what they were collectively brought up to believe.

—Richard Dawkins—Time to Stand Up,
written for the Freedom From Religion Foundation,
Sept. 2001.

Why Science Works and Why Religion Fails

Given the natural phenomena of human intelligence and consciousness, it is not difficult to understand why different people see and understand the world we live in in different contexts. Even though the world and the cosmos are objective and knowable, different opinions are derived from different interpretations of reality. The world is not always what it seems to be; seeing "eye-to-eye" and coming to the same conclusions is the exception, not the rule. Therefore, it would seem that having a model or paradigm for assessing the physical and the factual of our experience that eliminates much of the highly variable subjectivity in our assessments and evaluations would be our highest priority. Such a paradigm would provide a means of determining the truth of a matter in a way that would compel nearly universal understanding and acceptance. Such a model would:

Require as much compelling, relevant evidence as can be assembled to assure well-grounded conclusions.

Demand that subsequent assertions of truth be capable of repeated verification/confirmation.

Demand external corroboration to guard against propaganda as a source of alleged truth.

Be receptive to and subject to continuous analysis and evaluation.

Be open ended and never final—non dogmatic, accommodate multiple perspectives and analyses, consider alternative viewpoints and explanations, and sift through all available evidence to arrive at the most reliable and dependable conclusions as possible.

Be a process that is democratic in concept and execution.

Regard all truths from this paradigm as a posteriori truths.

Make all new knowledge public forthwith.
Be based on methodological naturalism, rationalism, logic and reason.
Produce clearly defined data.
Provide reliable findings which have cognitive substance and merit.

When subjective distortions and speculative obfuscations are minimized in the decision-making process, clarity of thought can be realized. Workable methods and solutions become the products. Truths become demonstrably true. Consensus and agreement on the findings become nearly universal. Disagreements stimulate further research. We call this paradigm science.

In contrast, the religious paradigm:

Is authoritarian/totalitarian and hierarchical in origin—not democratic.
Is based on faith and revelation—no supporting evidence is demanded.
Does not require confirmation/verification of claims or assertions.
Does not require external corroboration of assertions.
Posits absolute/final truth that has been determined arbitrarily.
Is based on a priori presuppositions.
Has been derived from a gossamer web of mystical, mythological, subjective, theological speculations and baseless conjecture.
Is not receptive to either internal or external evaluation or criticism.
Is dogmatic and doctrinaire—inflexible and strongly tends to be static.
Discounts logic, reason, and rationality.
Is devoid of data.
Has neither cognitive substance nor merit.

As a consequence, the claims and assertions of religion lack anything resembling a sound foundation, lack confirmable or verifiable information, and are prone to irrationality, unreason and illogical conclusions.

In the religious paradigm, resolution of different or contrasting views is very difficult to nearly impossible because there is nothing substantive on which to base a conclusion. All views are devoid of anything concrete and are purely subjective. The result is that resolution of different interpretations is virtually impossible without an absolute and arbitrary authority. This means that all authority is vested in and held by the king or the priest/bishop. The end result is tyranny, bloodshed, death and a return to the Dark Ages.

In any venue of rigorous intellectual disputation, a model or paradigm for determining the truth of a matter is necessary. In the absence of a third option, the clear choice between the scientific paradigm and the religious paradigm for truth telling about anything of the physical and the factual is science.

We must never retreat in the face of threats or punishments dispensed by theocratic terrorists more interested in protecting their power and indulging their vanity, than in advancing the human condition. If, as the true believers claim, the word 'gospel' means good news, then the good news for me is that there is no gospel, other than what I can define for myself, by observation and conscience. As a freethinking human being, I have come not to favor or fear religion, but to face and fight it as an impediment to civilized advancement.

—Steve Benson,
"From Latter-Day Saint to Latter-Day Ain't"
(1999),

~~~~~~~~~~~~~~~~~~

In the long run nothing can withstand reason and experience, and the contradiction religion offers to both is only too palpable.

—Sigmund Freud (1856-1939),
"The Future of an Illusion"
(1927)

~~~~~~~~~~~~~~~~~~

Religious bondage shackles and debilitates the mind and unfits it for every noble enterprise.

—President James Madison

The King, The Priest and We The People

From the beginning there were the king and the priest. This was (and is in some places) the original power play employed by the more assertive or aggressive men in the tribe. These were the "Alpha" people. These were the men whose appetite for power grew from their desire to have dominion over others—the "Beta" people and lesser folk. They rose to their position of power by guile, persuasion, charisma, intimidation and as often as not by physical force.

The maintenance of their position in the hierarchical society was always tentative because there were always men who were envious of the power and authority of the king and the priest. Enforcing their rule occupied much of their time and attention. Such is the nature of men.

Along with the consciousness and intelligence that evolved as features of the human brain was the need to have answers to their questions. Humans have a need to know what is right and good from what is wrong and not good. Unlike other animals whose behavior is largely governed by instinct, the long period of time for maturation of humans requires an education of the young by their parents and the elders of the tribe. Answers have to come from someone.

Maintaining the status quo is very much in the interests of the ruling class. Stability, constancy and predictability in the social structure was a high priority. Social cohesion was a necessity for survival. The ignorant masses sought answers from their ruling class. As often as not those answers were supplied whether questions were asked or not. If questions arose for which the ruling class did not have answers, then answers were created as needed by those in power. This was the origin of revealed truth. When those answers worked, the masses followed docilely. When those answers did not work, there was unrest and instability—even rebellion.

The ignorance that was always the source of fear of the unknown and the unpredictable has always been and still is the reason people are in a near constant state of anxiety. Consequently, accepting the explanations of those in authority as to what is true and what is not, what is acceptable and what is not, becomes a social standard for nearly everyone. Whether those answers are rational and intellectually defensible becomes subordinated to maintaining the status quo. "The Word" comes from "On High."

To argue that there are other explanations or alternative views is to challenge the authority from "On High." This provokes more questions and divisiveness. Authority figures find this intolerable. To question authority figures or to challenge them is declared blasphemy and is deemed a capitol offense. Death or banishment to those who disagree or challenge authority figures was the rule.

Revealed truth is and has always been whatever those in power decided was the truth about any matter. The king and the priest, who invent whatever god suits their purpose, invoke divine sanction to support their tenuous tenure. Their primary tools are fear, guilt, shame, and sin. They decide what is to be their dogma and doctrine. They decide how people are to think, what people are to believe, and how they are to behave. All dissent is crushed. The psychological manipulation of the masses through promises of heaven and threats of hell has been the tool of choice for the kings and the priests for all of human history. Regrettably, it has been a remarkably successful strategy.

In an evolutionary context this has produced human beings who are prone to being believers and followers. This has been adaptive as it has been responsible for much of the social cohesion that was necessary for survival. The status quo has had its advantages, but it severely inhibits cultural advance that is dependent on innovation and alternate views of reality. The status quo also tends to strongly stifle creativity and cultural evolution.

This kind of governance has been the near universal modus operandi for all human cultures for all of human history. Then the most profound paradigm shift in human history happened. The Americans—the restless masses in an English colony—decided they would demand a different kind of governance. They rebelled against the authority of the king and the priest (Bishop) and rejected all authority, both secular and ecclesiastical of the historic power brokers who had tyrannized the masses for all of human history. Then they created a secular republic whose constitution began, "We the People . . . ."

Who burnt heretics? Who roasted or drowned millions of 'witches'? Who built dungeons and filled them? Who brought forth cries of agony from honest men and women that rang to the tingling stars? Who burnt Bruno? Who spat filth over the graves of Paine and Voltaire? The answer is one word—Christians.

—G.W. Foote. "Are Atheists Wicked?,"
chapter from Flowers of Freethought (1894)

~~~~~~~~~~~~~~~~~

I am now convinced that children should not be subjected to the frightfulness of the Christian religion . . . . If the concept of a father who plots to have his own son put to death is presented to children as beautiful and as worthy of society's admiration, what types of human behavior can be presented to them as reprehensible.

—Ruth Hurmence Green, Preface of "Born Again
Skeptic's" Guide to the Bible.

~~~~~~~~~~~~~~~~~

When a religion is good, I conceive it will support itself; and when it does not support itself, and God does not take care to support it so that its professors are obliged to call for help of the civil power, 'tis a sign, I apprehend, of its being a bad one.

—Benjamin Franklin, Works, Vol. XIII, p. 506

Gods, Power and the Origin of Religions

In human history there have been thousands of religions, and more than 20,000 gods are counted in our libraries. Among religious believers we frequently encounter assertions that their favorite god is the One True God, and all others are false. Since all but one of these assertions must be wrong, we are left with only one option, and that is to identify the One True God without any external help. An appearance by the One True God would certainly be helpful in our quest—alas, not one has been forthcoming. Just think how many lives would be spared since we would all know who the One True God would be, and we would all understand that god in the same context. Hence, we would not feel compelled to slaughter those whose One True God was a competitor of our One True God.

In the absence of an appearance of a One True God in our time, we are left to our own devices to choose a religion from those that are extant. Those religions that survive only as historical memes present an intellectual problem since we don't have any hard evidence to verify the existence of any of their gods. We cannot place any more credibility in one set of religious myths, metaphors, allegories, and symbols than any other. It logically follows then that all religions are equally valid or invalid. The claims or assertions of one tribe are just as worthy or unworthy as those of any other. Mystical, mythological narratives citing miracles and other fantastical tales that defy and deny the known laws of the universe from one culture are no more credible than those of any other.

Since all of the religions and competing gods are contradictory, and we have no means of making an informed choice among them, we are left with the conclusion that all religions are equally invalid as intellectually defensible options. Religions that cannot stand up to rigorous examination and critical, scholarly evaluation fail to provide a format or platform on which we can construct a credible and valid world view. Hence, educated people tend to strongly eschew organized religions as the religions fail the test of reality. For instance, 93% of the members of the National Academy of Sciences do not subscribe to any of the organized monotheistic religions.

Of course, there are always those self-appointed and self-authenticating "messengers" whose unconstrained zeal, coupled with their pious sincerity, seduce the credulous and gullible unthinking masses who accept the propaganda of the purveyor of "The Truth." However, personal anecdotal narratives or other information from a single source (propaganda) has never stood the test of time as a reliable source of truth. Religions have a long track record of regarding skepticism, scrutiny, and analysis as dangerously subversive behavior that must be crushed forthwith lest it inspire evaluation against reality and result in social unrest.

The reality of nature coupled with higher order thinking skills, academic honesty and intellectual integrity brings on the demise of organized religions. Religions prosper and continue to exist only when ignorance, superstition and magical thinking prevail as the dominant philosophical paradigm in the mind of the public.

Every word, every sentence, paragraph, and story in every religious text or oral tradition has originated in the mind of a man who was determined to superimpose his will and views on other people. The king and the priest solidified their position of power by declaring that their views had the sanction of a supernatural god, and that any challenge to that authority was heresy and therefore punishable by death. Dissenters who remained were labeled as blasphemers and executed, or they packed up their wives and children and headed into the wilderness with whoever would follow them. This, it is reasonable to believe, was a significant cause of the dispersal of human beings across the face of the earth.

Power-hungry men with their unmitigated ignorance of the natural phenomena of their world and their boundless hubris were the source of "The Word of God." Men, in all of their ignorance, and with all of their failings, unwarranted biases, and irrational prejudices were the source of "The Word of God." Men, not gods, whose appetite for power, control, and dominion over others, were the source of "The Word of God." The "Word of God" was whatever the prevailing triumvirate of the king and the priest and their "God" said it was. It has always been so. The powers that are in control are still suppressing and killing dissenters—literally and figuratively.

The monotheistic religions conceived in a tribal cultural milieu, and borne of abject fear and complete ignorance of all we have learned in the last two thousand years, can hardly be regarded as an appropriate paradigm from which we can derive ethical and moral codes in our time and place in history. In the absence of any revealed truth from any omniscient deity in our time, we are compelled to employ the most sophisticated minds among us, and in a democratic context to compose our own ethical and moral codes from our own history and experience that will be judged by their consequences in our time.

And so it goes—with "God" as the ultimate subjectivity, open to an infinite number of interpretations by an infinite number of people, some with altruistic motives and some with nefarious motives borne of the ambitions of megalomaniacal tyrants, we are sliding pell-mell into a philosophical black hole from which nothing but disaster can result.

The monotheistic religions, Judaism, Christianity, and Islam, all conceived and derived from an ancient, tribal world view, by ambitious egotists who arrogantly called themselves "prophets" and labeled their control paradigm as the sacred word of their god, were conceived in and derived from a profound ignorance of the cause and effect of the natural phenomena that so profoundly influenced their lives.

Any world view, secular or religious, that is to serve as a model for our ethical and moral codes must of necessity be founded on and derived from a world view that is consistent with a modern, scientific understanding of the world and the cosmos. Objectivity, reason, logic, and finely honed critical thinking skills for solving our problems in our time, must supplant any religiously inspired world view if we are to avoid the continued repetition of the catastrophic failures of the monotheistic religions that have dominated our thinking for more than 2000 years.

The lessons learned from the dinosaurs are clear and unambiguous—evolve and adapt to the modern, changing realities of our time, or become extinct.

The Old Testament is responsible for more atheism, agnosticism, disbelief—call it what you will—than any book ever written; it has emptied more churches than all the counter-attractions of cinema, motor bicycle and golf course.

—A.A. Milne, cited in "2,000 Years of Disbelief."

~~~~~~~~~~~~~~~~~~

The merits and services of Christianity have been industriously extolled by its hired advocates. Every Sunday its praises are sounded from myriads of pulpits. It enjoys the prestige of an ancient establishment and the compre-hensive support of the State. It has the ear of rulers and the control of education. Every generation is suborned in its favor. Those who dissent from it are losers, those who oppose it are ostracized; while in the past, for century after century, it has replied to criticism with imprisonment, and to skepticism with the dungeon and the stake. By such means it has induced a general tendency to allow its pretensions without inquiry and its beneficence without proof.

—Preface, "Crimes of Christianity,"
by G.W. Foote and J.M. Wheeler.

The Ten Revolutionary Changes That Human Beings Must Make to Avoid Possible Extinction in the 21st Century.

Proposing or introducing change of any kind will make many people nervous and uncomfortable. Some people will actually react to change in a hostile manner. People with a conservative mind set are those most likely to become upset over proposed change. Change is anathema to conservatives. Believing conservatives who say they are agents of reform is like believing that a fox is an appropriate guardian of your chickens. No one wants chaos, but liberals are those who are most likely to be comfortable with uncertainty, ambiguity, paradox and the intellectual challenge of change. Reform promulgated by liberals, however, is always necessary because the status quo to which conservatives cling so desperately is a kind of intellectual as well as a social malignancy that suffocates cultural advance.

At this point in human history the monotheistic religions, Judaism, Christianity, and Islam, have been a conservative cultural meme for many centuries. Conceived in the ignorance of all that humankind has learned about ourselves and the cosmos in these many centuries and frozen in time, these ancient and archaic paradigms have outlived any usefulness they might have had and do not serve the best interests of humankind. It would be of little matter today if these cultural relics were benign in their influence on human society, but on the contrary, they are insidiously divisive and so destructive that they must be abandoned and relegated to our libraries as cultural artifacts that have failed to evolve apace with human intellectual and cultural advance.

Since all religions are attempts to understand and explain our relationship with nature, and since the religious paradigm has a long record of abject failure in this regard, we are best advised to employ a different paradigm that takes into account the expanded knowledge base that has accrued in the last several centuries. Our understanding of natural phenomena is now best explained by the scientific paradigm. Religions are based on purely subjective, mystical, mythological speculation and unsupported conjecture. In our modern, high tech, scientific age the religious paradigm does not satisfy our need for dependable, reliable truth about natural phenomena.

The scientific paradigm has deep roots in the intellectual history of Western Civilization that goes all the way back to ancient Greece. It is interesting to speculate as to what extent science might have advanced by this date if the societal cancer of the Roman Catholic Church had not induced a thousand years of cultural and intellectual stagnation called The Dark Ages.

Modern science has a history that goes back to Roger Bacon, (circa 1214-1294), who was an early advocate of empiricism—knowledge acquired through experience as opposed to doctrine or revelation. Other advocates of empiricism who came later were Hobbes, Locke, Hume and Mill.

Today the scientific intellectual enterprise is the most dependable and reliable means of truth telling known to humans. While science does not pretend to answer all of our questions, its methods demand evidentiary support for all truth claims that must be confirmed or verified, supported by external corroboration and be receptive to ongoing review, scrutiny, analysis, and evaluation. Modern society and culture are predicated, founded and supported entirely on the scientific approach to understanding and the explication of natural phenomena.

All scientific truths are regarded as a posteriori truths that are derived after experimentation or other objective research. Science attempts to learn about natural phenomena by first observing nature and then arriving at what is regarded as truth by logical inference and deductions that are consistent with the relevant data.

In contrast, "religious truths" are a priori conclusions that have been superimposed on nature. As regards natural phenomena, the religious paradigm has a long, bloody history of demonstrable failure. It is amazing that the monotheistic religions have survived as long as they have in the light of a modern knowledge base. Warm, soft, fuzzy myths apparently are still preferred by most people to the cold, hard realities of living one's life on earth.

While our myths are still, and probably always will be, a substantial part of the social glue that holds human society together, we are now at a point that demands that ancient, archaic, mystical, mythological, subjective speculation and unsupported conjectures be relegated to the dustbin of history as explanatory models. In its place new stories based on the modern, scientific understanding of natural phenomena must be composed and must prevail. Human survival in the 21st century literally depends on this profound paradigm shift. The monotheistic religions, as they are constituted and promulgated, are the most dangerous, divisive, and baleful influences in the world today. More people have been, and still are being, slaughtered under the aegis of faith-based initiatives than all other human causes.

Given the egregious philosophical errors of the monotheistic religions that are a demonstrable failure for life guidance, human survival beyond the 21st century will necessitate a new Renaissance and a new Enlightenment that are grounded in a humanistic, scientific paradigm. The all-too-human propensity for absolutist, authoritarian, totalitarian behavior with alleged divine sanction must be completely replaced by an ethical/moral code derived from a secular, scientific, rational understanding of ourselves and our world if human beings are to have a future beyond the 21st century.

Will this revolutionary paradigm shift come soon? NO! The seemingly human addiction to supernatural religions must be replaced by a rational, unifying, intellectually defensible world view that serves all people. The public debate on the merits of a new global paradigm must start now if there is to be substantial change by the end of the century. If this necessary change in how we define ourselves and our future as a species on this planet does not start very soon it will be very unlikely it can be realized at all. It will take a Herculean educational effort that will cost billions of dollars. All of this cost can be covered by extracting it from the budget of the Pentagon's war machine.

Nature has not given us any guarantee that the human race will survive in perpetuity on this planet. On the contrary—biological history has shown conclusively that all species are destined to evolutionary extinction. We have no reason to even imagine that we are exempt from the laws of nature.

The issue before us now is: Will the extinction of human beings come sooner or later? At the present and accelerating rate of human population growth, and the insatiable demands for the world's finite resources, we are on a steep and slippery slope to self extermination.

Following are the ten revolutionary ideas that human beings must change to avoid possible extinction in the 21st century. This is an incomplete list, but these are the most pressing issues facing us that require resolution before we address other issues. Ancient, archaic, obsolete ideas and ideologies must be replaced by a modern assessment, analysis, and evaluation of our philosophical positions if we are to survive as a species and conserve our planet for posterity.

Deities

The ancient and archaic idea that gods are real or that they matter in any way in human affairs must be abandoned. Gods are the product of human imagination and have no place in the thinking of intelligent, appropriately educated people. Gods were created by barbaric Stone Age thinking and handed down from generation to generation as cultural memes that may have served an evolutionary function in Stone Age cultures, but today they are maladaptive, and believing in them as realities is patently dangerous. Of the 20,000 or so gods of record from thousands of human cultures—all are mythological and none of them have any more veracity than any other. There is no justification to favoring any one of them over another. Gods of any kind, whether one believes in one or many, are not only inconsistent with, but are contradictory to, a modern knowledge base. While our cultural myths support and help define who and what we are, modern stories that are consistent with our modern knowledge base must be created, and archaic myths must be discarded as they are obsolete and inappropriate for us in our time and do not serve our needs.

In all of human history, invoking a deity to explain natural phenomena is how ignorant people explain what they don't understand.

We conclude that gods are the measure of our desperation, and theologies are the measure of our gullibility.

Saviors

Man/God hero figures and "Saviors" as agents for "salvation" are myths of a time and culture that is so alien to our contemporary intellectual culture that such an idea today is not only incomprehensible, it is absurd. Such hero figures arose from the myths of scores of ancient cultures. None of them, no matter how appealing, has ever stood up to critical examination. They are all fictive accounts by the more imaginative folk who wanted to create an idealistic icon that they could worship and follow, because their leaders, the real people among them, were seriously flawed and fallible human beings who were prone to error and extraordinarily cruel toward others. The icon of an omnibenevolent transcendent savior is very appealing to the ignorant, the credulous and the naive, but in the light of a modern knowledge base, it is a baseless lie. Our salvation (whatever that means), either individually or collectively, is in our hands, and we should not and cannot expect any help from any alleged external source. Children should be educated to the modern realities of our existence, not indoctrinated with pie-in-the-sky archaic myths that have been proffered by overly zealous priests as factual history.

Heaven and Hell

The phenomenon of human consciousness provides a level of self awareness that enables humans to understand that at some point they will die like every other living thing on this planet. Consequently, the most abhorrent abstract concept of all human thought is that inevitable death will bring total annihilation and complete oblivion. This is what all human beings fear above all else. The most universal desire in human experience is that their essence—their psyche—their being—their spirit, will somehow be able to survive the death of their body. Death denial has assumed a variety of forms in human experience—witness the embalming and preservation of human bodies as long ago as the early Egyptians—5000 years ago. The barbaric idea of an afterlife assuredly goes back far into prehistory.

The idea of an existence in an after life in an idealized place that is free from the trials, tribulations, and painful reality in this vale of tears most certainly is the most attractive idea to ever spring from the imagination of human beings. The fact that no one has ever returned from such a place after death and no confirmation has ever been provided by anyone to verify the existence of such a wonderful place has not inhibited people one bit from desperately clinging to such an idea. Humans have always clung to irrational ideas that they found attractive and comfortable; they always will.

Various people from disparate cultures around the world have imagined and even created visual images of what such an idealized place might look like. Some have imagined that such a place was above the clouds or on top of an unclimbable sacred mountain.

The more imaginative people in a given culture (more than likely the king or the ubiquitous priest) made political capital of this phenomenon and with their dualistic thinking created the dichotomy of heaven and hell as a tool for rewards and punishment in an afterlife. Heaven and Hell are intellectual constructs created by priests as reward and punishment ideas to control the ignorant, restless masses. In our history they have been powerful ideas that have been used to manipulate the ignorant and the credulous. Heaven and hell, while never having passed any test of reality are still a part of the mythology of millions of people.

In our time and in our culture the ideas of heaven and hell may serve the purposes of grossly ignorant people, but for appropriately educated people such ideas have no more veracity than children's fairy tales and consequently are not a part of their thinking. Indoctrinating children with the ideas of heaven and hell interferes with their ability to accurately assess reality and corrupts their cognitive processes. Child abuse is a crime.

Satan

The idea of Satan or the Devil as a kind of demigod that presides over the domain of Hell is pure mythology created by priests to explain why their benevolent all-powerful god doesn't really have omnipotent power over all things. When things go bad there has to be some way of explaining to the ignorant masses why their god could not deliver what was desired. There has to be someone or something (the scapegoat) to blame. After all, God can't be held accountable for all of the misfortune in the world. If God is omniscient and omnipotent and various natural phenomena (tsunamis, tornadoes, floods, earthquakes, et. al.) devastate the area, someone has to bear the blame, hence Satan, the mythological fall guy. When people behave badly they can always cop out by blaming the Devil.

Fear, guilt, shame, sin and death have been the message of the priest to the ignorant masses. These are the tools of the game of control, and Satan has always been a convenient idea for those in power whose appetite for dominion over others has no limits.

There are better ways to teach children (regardless of their age) how to understand and govern their lives in a social context than with ancient and archaic tactics that do not address themselves to modern contingencies. A modern understanding and interpretation of our lives leaves no room for such monstrous and egregious intellectual errors as Satan. In the absence of any compelling evidence as to the existence of a Devil or Satan, we are best advised to divest ourselves and our culture of such a barbarous and intellectually indefensible idea.

Angels and Demons

In a modern scientific understanding of natural phenomena there is no justification for believing in any sort of angels or demons.

Such ideas are the fictive creations of ignorant people. Ideas born of ignorance and fear have no place in the intellectual endeavors of educated people.

Monotheistic Revealed Religions

The monotheistic Abrahamic revealed religions, Judaism, Islam, and Christianity, are archaic cultural artifacts (memes) that are now obsolete in our modern scientific culture. They no longer serve our collective best interests. All three are grounded in and founded on a profound misunderstanding and misinterpretation of natural phenomena. Consequently, they are now known to be riddled with egregious intellectual errors that cannot be a part of modern thinking for educated people. Created in an alien culture and frozen in time, these static world views derived and constructed in total ignorance of all we have learned about ourselves and the cosmos in the last 2000 years are not and cannot be an appropriate source or guide for us in our culture and in our time. Contemporary community standards of our modern ethical and moral codes are sharply at odds with the archaic standards that were derived from ancient texts that were arbitrarily deemed to be sacred. Any religion that expects to remain viable must evolve with a rapidly evolving culture; otherwise it becomes dated, obsolete and loses its credibility. This is what has happened. This is why these three religions have lost membership among the more educated of the world's people.

The paradigm of absolutist religions produces authoritarian regimes which inevitably descends into totalitarianism. The intolerance inherent in totalitarianism results in the exacerbation of xenophobia and bigotry which cascades into persecution and the violence of genocide and murder. This is antithetical to democratic governance.

When people have been led to believe that they have an absolute truth from an Absolute Authority, they have swung the doors to disaster wide open. Religious certainty borne of absolute truth and coupled with religious conviction is the most dangerous—indeed the most lethal combination in human history. Blaise Pascal wrote, "Men never do evil so completely and cheerfully as when they do it from religious conviction." More people have been persecuted, tortured and killed as a consequence of religious certitude than for any other cause. The Crusades, The Inquisition, The Holocaust, the jihads, the fatwas, the pogroms, the witch hunts, and countless other atrocities against humankind were all derived directly from religious absolutism and certainty.

The Bible

What is the Bible? In spite of some of its positives, it is a collection of ancient, primordial visions and poetical figments of archaic imaginations. It reflects traditional tribal prejudices, subjective distortions, verbal confusions and intellectual obfuscations of an alien cultural zeitgeist. It was written in near total ignorance of the physical and biological laws of the universe. It has been superseded by an expanded human knowledge base that has accrued in the past 2000 years.

The Bible is riddled with numerous inconsistencies, countless contradictions, and it defies a coherent understanding and interpretation of its message even by those who claim to know it best. It contains scores of metaphors, allegorical narratives, and symbolic references that were written in the context of the culture extant at that time. Most of these are poorly understood, if not completely misunderstood, by those who claim to have a firm grip on a comprehensive understanding of the text. Others assert a very different perspective and interpretation.

The Bible was written by people (men only) who were more concerned with providing "pictures for the mind" for the illiterate masses than with the intellectual disputations so characteristic of modern explication and scholarship.

The Bible contains scores of interpolations, redactions, errors of fact, muddled chronologies and copyists errors. Historically, it is a mishmash at best. Many of its meanings and lessons have been lost, distorted, or misinterpreted in translation from languages that have evolved contextually from the original editions.

The Bible is riddled with calculated ambiguities, literary tricks, smudgy semantic stratagems, ecclesiastical politics and an unhealthy dose of religious zealotry. All of this confusion is contained in a tome that is supposed to inspire, lead and advise us.

The Bible has been examined, scrutinized, analyzed, and interpreted, ad infinitum, for centuries by professionals and lay persons alike and still defies a clarified view of what is and what ought to be, especially for our time and our cultural circumstances.

It has been alleged that it is the "Word of God," which is an ancient and often used assertion made by priests to lend authority to their ideas that they wanted to superimpose on the willful masses, even though no evidentiary support has ever been proffered to support that assertion.

The Bible sanctions the beating of children, slavery, ownership of concubines (sex slaves), and it regards women as property (like livestock) and casts them as second class citizens. All of these, and many more, are totally at odds with our contemporary community standards.

The Bible demands the death penalty (by stoning or strangulation) for a long list of offenses such as working on the Sabbath or disrespecting one's parents even if they have been violently abusive. Messages of love and compassion are severely compromised and contradicted. Messages from a sacred text should be consistent and internally coherent.

The priestly assertion that the Bible is the word of an omniscient and omnipotent god is probably the most intellectually indefensible statement of all time. Only a modicum of scholarship and some attentive evaluation clearly expose the inconsistencies and contradictions that could not exist in a tome inspired by an omniscient god.

Unequivocally, the Bible—an obsolete artifact derived from an alien culture—is inappropriate as a sacred icon and guide in our time.

Faith as a Source of Truth—Fideism

Saul of Tarsus, a.k.a. Saint Paul, allegedly wrote in his letter to the Hebrews 11:1, "Now, faith is the assurance of things hoped for, the conviction of things not seen." Somewhat paraphrased, this short verse reads: "One can regard with certainty whatever one wants without any supporting evidence." Of course this kind of thinking is completely at odds with modern ideas about how to solve problems. Further, such thinking is so alien to contemporary ideas of truth seeking that it would be condemned as cognitively worthless and thrown out of any modern court of law. So much for "The Word of God."

Given the ability of the human brain to think rationally, the blind faith of revealed religions is the negation of our humanity and is therefore immoral.

In a world that burgeons with chaos, superstition, fear, ambiguity, uncertainty, and ignorance there are two kinds of people: those who seek to understand through critical thinking, science, and rationality (higher intellectual function) and those who try to cope with the illusions of faith, denial and the irrationalities of revealed religion. If faith is acting on the nobler hypothesis, the nobler hypothesis can never contain untestable, unverifiable or unfalsifiable assertions.

Faith is an intellectual cop-out. With faith you can excuse or evade the necessity of evaluating evidence. Faith is belief without any corroborating evidence, without any confirmation or verification of any kind. If one finds truth by faith, then one can believe in and justify anything no matter how absurd, irrational or illogical. One can justify murder, war, and genocide. All of these things have been done. This is called sin. Truth by faith? The words credulous and gullible come to mind.

Belief, or faith, is the avowal of policy. If policies are based on logical, rational assertions that are supported by compelling evidence that can be verified or confirmed, then beliefs can have merit. Such beliefs can be employed to advantage in the decision-making process that can benefit everyone. If policies do not or cannot meet the above criteria, then beliefs made from these policies are flawed in such a way and to such an extent that decisions made based on such beliefs are most likely to be against the best interest of everyone. This is why faith-based policies and subsequent beliefs are so prone to disastrous results. Societal and cultural catastrophes occur when ideologies take precedence over our reason and critical thinking skills.

Mythology as History

When we were school children we learned about the mythologies of the Romans, the Greeks, the Egyptians, the Norse, the Persians, the indigenous Americans and others. They were taught as myths and we understood them to be myths—not factual history. We learned about the role myths played in evolving human cultures.

In contrast, however, from very early in Christian history, the Roman Catholic Church insisted that the Hebrew myths were historically factual and they were taught as such. This policy continues to this day. There is no reason to believe that ancient Hebrew Biblical myths were historically truer than those from any other culture. The Protestant Reformation did nothing to refute and correct this egregious intellectual error.

Religious narratives were written by priests with an ideological agenda. They were not written by academic historians who were trying dispassionately to create an objective, factual record of the past. People who are prone to a literalist/fundamentalist interpretation of a mystical, mythological, allegorical narrative are making a profound intellectual error that distorts and confuses the message intended. Religious messages shrouded in the fog of subjective obfuscation cannot be an efficacious means of providing guidance for the masses.

Religious messages that are not clear create confusion and consequently are the source of a kind of misunderstanding that often proves to be extraordinarily dangerous.

Salvation

For most people the concept of salvation involves surviving the death of one's body in the context of a sanctioned mode and environment. Of course, surviving the death of one's body in any context is a barbaric and intellectually insupportable idea that is completely delusional. However, people have always had a strong predilection to prefer warm, fuzzy irrationalities to cold, hard rationalities.

Because the concepts of heaven and hell are purely priest craft tools for the manipulation of the ignorant, credulous masses, and are contradictory to the known laws of the earth and the cosmos, educated people do not regard them as credible ideas. Hence, entertaining the idea of salvation will have to be only in the context of the here and now of people's lives. In the 21st century any concept of salvation will, of necessity, be realized with an expansive modern, scientific knowledge base, a skeptical approach regarding the claims and assertions of others, well developed higher order critical thinking skills, and a philosophy that is receptive to new knowledge. Getting or making the most out of one's life will be derived from the highest possible development of one's intellectual potential, not from accepting and believing as true someone else's subjective, unverifiable, theological speculations.

The intellectual flaws and egregious errors in the subjective religious paradigm, that unfortunately dominates the thinking of the public at large and especially the leadership that establishes policy at all levels of our government, are so profound that they preclude arriving at workable solutions to our problems. In lieu of the religious paradigm for society as a whole and governing bodies in particular, a secular, scientific, objective paradigm derived from higher order thinking skills and an expanded modern knowledge base must be sanc-tioned and promulgated as public policy if human beings are to effectively govern themselves at all levels. If this change does not take place, the continuation of the religious paradigm which has resulted in an irresolvable intellectual quagmire born of subjective religious certitude and unsubstantiated theological speculation will result in an accelerating decline that will exacerbate the increasingly serious problems that threaten civilization as we know it. The worldwide catastrophic collapse of society, even the near extinction of the human race before the end of the twenty first century is possible unless the above changes are implemented.

I can indeed hardly see how anyone ought to wish Christianity to be true; for if so the plain language of the text seems to show that the men who do not believe, and this would include my Father, Brother, and almost all my best friends, will be everlastingly punished. And this is a damnable doctrine.

—Charles Darwin, Autobiography

~~~~~~~~~~~~~~~~~~~

Your book drove away the constraint of my old superstition, as if it had been a nightmare.

—Sir Francis Galton, (Cousin of Charles Darwin)
letter to Darwin, recorded in Life and
Letters of F. Galton (1914)

Ten Criteria For Believing

Of all the ideas that we have been asked to believe, few have ever been an effective filter for deciding if the claims or assertions of others have merit. Faced with a modern media blitz and information overload from so many sources, it is often difficult to separate the wheat from the chaff. It seems as though someone is always trying to sell us on their version of the truth. Almost invariably it is in their interests, not ours.

In an historical and evolutionary context it has been adaptive for humans to be believers of the claims and assertions of leaders. Without this innate propensity to believe charismatic leaders, there would be little chance for the level of social cohesion so necessary for survival of our species. Human beings, in spite of their superior intellect, would have had very little chance of survival as a species in the early stages of their existence as free roaming individuals. In a modern context, this natural inclination to be a believer of the claims or assertions presented to us with sincerity and enthusiasm, by people with an appetite for power, is a double edged sword. "Believing" can be both richly rewarding and catastrophically expensive.

Some guidelines or criteria for being selective and discriminating about what we should believe seem to be in order.

First, a skeptical attitude toward all claims and assertions by others is well advised. Otherwise, we are easily victimized by the unprincipled and the immoral. The history of human beings has been the history of the few who would exploit the many for their personal gain. Credulous fools are always the easy victims of unscrupulous predators.

We should always keep in the front of our minds a demand for compelling evidence in support of any claim or assertion. Without this compelling evidence, such unsupported claims or assertions have neither value nor merit, are therefore cognitively worthless and consequently not worthy of our consideration.

Verification or confirmation of claims and assertions is necessary for establishing the truth of a proposal. Without verification or confirmation, claims or assertions are unsubstantiated and represent intellectual or emotional traps that can be very expensive, even lethal.

A single source of information, proposals, propositions, claims and assertions for which no external corroboration can be presented are nothing more than propaganda, whether from a newspaper or a holy book. Placing credibility in these attempts at persuasion puts one at extreme risk. The fact that these attempts to persuade are in print, on film, or on television, gives them no more credibility than if they were in the temporal nature of speech.

Personal anecdotal narratives, testimonials, eyewitness accounts and popularly held opinions have been notoriously unreliable sources of truth. Sincerity coupled with enthusiasm has always been the most effective tool of persuasion by con artists.

Allegedly "sacred texts" are largely frozen in time in an ancient cultural milieu and are consequently outdated and obsolete for us in our time and culture. Any religion or other ideology must evolve fast enough with the advances in our culture and knowledge base to remain relevant and significant in our modern lives. We should therefore regard such "sacred texts" as archaic cultural artifacts that are products of human history and belong in our libraries as references to the thinking and the values and practices of our ancient, past.

Any proposal, proposition, claim or assertion that is presented in a manner that makes an appeal to our emotions should be regarded with extreme skepticism. The purveyors of these attempts at persuasion are using an age-old method of over ruling our intellect before we decide our course of action. Unfortunately, they have been and continue to be very successful at exploiting the gullible and the credulous among us. With very few exceptions their persuasion will cost people money that they willingly give these social criminals.

Mystical, mythological, allegorical narratives from any source cannot be understood as historical fact no matter who promulgates them as such. Such stories that deny and defy the known laws of the universe are outside the realm of the physical and the factual and must be considered and taught in a mythological, not a factual or historical context.

"Authority figures" of any kind or description have a long history of being either partially or totally wrong. Therefore, all truths should be regarded as tentative, provisional, and subject to revision or rejection as valid truths.

Any claim, assertion, myth, legend, story, proposition, proposal, policy or law from any source that is presented as an absolute truth should be regarded as fatally flawed. The lessons of history are replete with countless examples of absolute truth that have proven, on examination and evaluation, to be false. Absolutist doctrines from authoritarian/ totalitarian regimes are antithetical to, as well as contradictory to, modern concepts of democracy, freedom of inquiry, academic honesty and intellectual integrity.

If we hold that our ethical and moral standards are founded upon unassailable authority (faith) that originated several thousand years ago in an alien tribal culture, we are at the same time declaring as useless all that we have learned about ourselves and the universe since that time. Is this wise?

It was, of course, a lie what you read about my religious convictions, a lie that is being systematically repeated. I do not believe in a personal God and I have never denied this, but have expressed it clearly. If there is something in me that can be called religious then it is the unbounded admiration for the structure of the world so far as our science can reveal it.

—Albert Einstein

~~~~~~~~~~~~~~~~~~

The idea of a being who interferes with the sequence of events in the world is absolutely impossible.

—Albert Einstein

~~~~~~~~~~~~~~~~~~

Faith and knowledge are related as the two scales of balance; when the one goes up, the other goes down . . . . The power of religious dogma, when inculcated early, is such as to stifle conscience, compassion, and finally every feeling of humanity . . . . For, as you know, religions are like glow worms; they shine only when it's dark. A certain amount of ignorance is the condition of all religions, the element in which alone they can exist.

—Arthur Schopenhauer, "Parerga and Paralipomena" (1851),
cited in Who's Who in Hell compiled by Warren Allen Smith

Liberty, Freedom, and Justice for All

In all of human history old ideas have been abandoned as new knowledge superseded obsolete ideas. This resulted in the changes that fed cultural growth, which is a cumulative process. This was the way of the world in the past, and is in the present. As long as there are intelligent beings on earth, it will be the way of the future. The problem for most people is that change of any kind is threatening because it introduces the element of the unknown and the unfamiliar. Conservatives are committed to the status quo and liberals embrace new knowledge, novelty, innovation, experimentation, and exploration. Hence, we find that it was the liberals who got us out of the caves and discovered that the earth is indeed a sphere.

Historically the conservatives have fought desperately to oppose the changes advanced by liberals. Racism and sexism that were formerly the cultural norm in nearly all societies have been drastically reduced by law. Slavery and women denied the right to vote are examples of obsolete ideas that have been relegated to the dustbin of history for good reasons. Social Security and Medicare are more recent examples of cultural advance that were advocated by liberals and were opposed by conservatives.

Now we have justifiable reasons to recognize that homosexuality is a common, natural biological phenomenon not only among humans, but throughout many different kinds of animals. Sexual orientation is not the black and white issue that many people have imagined it to be. Genetic determinism is a greater factor in the lives of humans than most people understand.

Sexual orientation is just as much of a genetic variable as skin color or eye color. To discriminate against a person whose sexual orientation is outside of the norm cannot be justified any more than discriminating against people with green eyes.

Today educated people seek answers for objectively understanding natural biological phenomena from the scientific paradigm—which has proven to be the most reliable means of truth telling about the physical and the factual to ever come from the minds of humans. Ancient and archaic ideas derived from the subjective speculation and unsupported conjecture of priests from an alien, pre-scientific culture cannot be expected to provide us with reliable knowledge in our modern time.

Those who would deny some people the liberty, freedom of choice, and their pursuit of happiness based on the obsolete ideas of an alien Zeitgeist from 2500 years ago are on the wrong side of history and need to get up to speed in the 21st century.

You find as you look around the world that every single bit of progress in humane feeling, every improvement in the criminal law, every step toward the diminution of war, every step toward better treatment of the colored races, or every mitigation of slavery, every moral progress that there has been in the world, has been consistently opposed by the organized churches of the world. I say quite deliberately that the Christian religion, as organized in its churches, has been and still is the principal enemy of moral progress in the world.

—Bertrand Russell, Why I am Not a Christian, 1927

~~~~~~~~~~~~~~~~~~

The truths of religion are never so well understood as by those who have lost their power of reasoning.

—Voltaire

Absolutism, Religious Fundamentalism, and Our Evolving Culture

So many ideas are multifaceted that getting a comprehensive understanding of these ideas requires broad vision and the ability to deal with myriad details. Few ideas are so simple that they can be grasped easily and adequately. Many ideas from religions may appear simplistic on the surface but internally may also carry veiled and complex concepts. Constructing a well-built bridge between themselves and a religious text can be a daunting task for the well informed, but is nearly impossible for less sophisticated people. Making meaning of their limited experience is a big problem for most people, and they seek external validation for who they are and what they perceive themselves to be.

People are prone to understanding and explaining complex ideas that are poorly understood in simplistic ways. The comprehensive explanation is more difficult to deal with, and if there is an easier way to incorporate the concepts into their little bag of answers, they are likely to take the easier path. Scholarship is very low on their list of priorities, intellectual discipline is outside of their frame of reference, and their mantra is: "Give it to me simple." Their uncritical thought results in arrested intellectual development that can ultimately lead to mind-numbing anti-intellectualism.

The easiest way to simplify a complex set of ideas is to polarize them into a small set of statements that reduces everything into a black and white picture—a kind of dualistic thinking. The dichotomies of: truth:falsehood; right:wrong; good:bad; God:Satan; heaven:hell; and us:them, are characteristic of the limited imaginations of such people. There is little tolerance for shades of gray which represent ambiguity and uncertainty. Neither is there room for, nor tolerance of, contradiction or paradox. Color and flavor represent cognitive complexity and multiple perspectives. They are anathema to the simplistic, fundamentalist view, and are avoided at all cost.

For the fundamentalists, the chosen authority figures are sources of truth, and all others are labeled as "false prophets" or "liberals" (used as a pejorative). Conformance, obedience, structure, ritual and membership in "approved" institutions are the necessary criteria. Learning is by rote memory (chapter and verse). Skepticism, inquiry and experimentation are strongly discouraged. Absolutism with "either/or" thinking and unquestioning acceptance of the word of authority figures further define the fundamentalist world view.

The academic honesty and intellectual integrity expected for genuine scholarship is subordinated, or eliminated entirely, for whatever is perceived to be convenient and comfortable. Emotional considerations have a higher priority than intellectual concerns, image triumphs over substance, and feelings trump rational thought. Thus, intellectual immaturity results in a simplistic, fundamentalist view of complex issues.

While the Bible, the Qu'ran, the Bhagavad Gita and other religious texts abound in metaphors, allegories and symbolism, the fundamentalist ignores, denies or fails to recognize the role these literary tools play in relating a story, a lesson, a parable, or a point of view. To the fundamentalist there is no such thing as a "veiled view" or a "hidden meaning." Fundamentalists seemingly fail to either appreciate or understand the profound differences in the cultural, political, economic and religious milieu of our time compared to those of Biblical times.

The fundamentalist fails to understand the distinction between numeracy and numerology; between poetry and prose; between the temporal and the spatial, between cosmology and astronomy, between syncretism and natural history, between chronology and theology, between myth and historical fact. Instead, the fundamentalist reads, interprets, and concludes everything on a strictly literal interpretation. They have been characterized as those who can see, but who have no vision. Of course, their conclusions are totally at odds with the intended message or with the lesson being taught. This is also known as the blind leading the blind. It is small wonder that Bishop John Shelby Spong referred to the untutored Bible study groups as "A pooling of ignorance." It becomes easy to understand why fundamentalism has been labeled as "Bonehead Theology" and "Neanderthal Religion" by well-educated people.

The fundamentalist, characterized by arrested cognitive development, adopts the absolutist mind set and is given to: avoiding intellectual adventures, condemning scientific research and experimentation, fits of exaggerated righteousness, resentment against the achievement of others, and endorsing conspiracy theorists and hate groups.

Their activities frequently involve compulsive church going, satanizing those who hold alternate views, giving religious testimonials, group hysteria, hyperbolic piety and militant proselytizing. Their tight circle of like minds tends strongly to be exclusionary and divisive.

It is tragic enough as it is that fundamentalists hold these socially crippling views, but the great tragedy for the public lies in the fact that these people cast a vote in our public elections. Equally as distressing, is that these irrational minds in positions of authority hand down public policy derived from absolutist ideologies. Ignorance compounded by stupidity extracts a terribly expensive price.

The ultimate tragedy results when the religious, absolutist/ extremist achieves great political power. Inevitably the consequences are bloodshed and wholesale death. History is replete with examples of religious absolutist horror such as: The Crusades, The Inquisition, the Muslim/Hindu atrocities, the Catholic/Protestant "unpleasantness" in Ireland, The Serbian/Croatian slaughters, the interminable Jewish/Muslim wars and the numerous Christian and Muslim conversion campaigns achieved at the point of a sword. Absolutism, whether derived from religion or secular ideologies, inevitably cascades into authoritarianism which cascades into totalitarianism. The abuse of power is the historical failing of humankind—we allow it at our peril.

Christian fundamentalists like Jerry Falwell, Pat Robertson, Jim Bakker, Jimmy Swaggart, Tim and Beverly LaHaye, Henry Morris, Duane Gish and a long list of other Biblical literalists who sincerely believe the intellectual claptrap that they parade as religion, have made a career of leading the naive, the gullible, and the credulous down a path of literalist ignorance. Along the way they have extracted millions of dollars from their prey. In their wake is a huge collection of the brains of their victims sucked dry, emptied, and devoid of any semblance of rational thought. Our Constitution guarantees their right to freedom of expression and that our government will not intrude on their right to practice their own brand of religious malignancy. It is like a license to steal without fear of prosecution. Fundamentalism from the charismatic, silver tongued mouths of unscrupulous predators can be very remunerative. P.T. Barnum was right when he said, "There is a sucker born every minute."

The self-imposed, willful, and invincible ignorance of the fundamentalist mind is a phenomenon that defies understanding, especially when it dominates the thinking of some reasonably intelligent people. Some people allege that this is symptomatic of the indelible brainwashing these people received as small children. The intellectual damage acquired in childhood can result in a lifelong handicap.

The lower order thinking skills of knowledge, comprehension and application are a part of the intellectual tools of all normal people. For the fundamentalist, this is usually as far as they get. The higher order thinking skills of analysis, synthesis, and evaluation are not the intellectual tools of the fundamentalist. Skepticism, evidentiary support for claims or assertions, experimentation and verification of claims so characteristic of higher order thinking skills, and modern problem solving skills are alien modes of thought to the fundamentalist. "The Bible says it—I believe it—that ends it!" is characteristic of the fundamentalist mind set. Genuine scholarship, which of necessity would employ higher order thinking skills, is not in the toolbox of fundamentalists. The denial of the legitimacy of genuine scholarship by fundamentalists is common if the findings of the scholarship are in contradiction to the previously held positions of most fundamentalists. Some people, even those with scientific credentials, have apparently managed to compartmentalize their brains to accommodate their fundamentalism, and isolate it from their science. Others have opined that since we have only one brain, fundamentalists have severely compromised their science when their bottom line thinking is, "God did it."

The license presumed by religious fundamentalists gives them free reign to subjectively derive anything they choose from their religious text. In so doing they can, and have, justified: environmental despoliation, racism, sexism, rape, murder, and genocide. The Nazi regime placed, "God is with us" on the inside of the belt buckle of the German soldiers. The xenophobic attitudes (us vs. them) so characteristic of the fundamentalist breeds intolerance (we are right, you are wrong) which leads to bigotry and demonization, which leads to hatred, persecution, and violence.

Jacob Bronowski was a Jew from Poland who emigrated to the United States and became an American citizen to escape the Holocaust. He was a mathematician, a physicist, a poet, a playwright, a humanitarian, a philosopher of science, and one of the intellectual giants of the 20th century, who wrote in his book, "The Ascent of Man.", "There is no absolute knowledge. And those who claim it, whether they are scientists or dogmatists, open the door to tragedy." This wisdom is confirmed by our experience and history.

Absolutism and its bastard offspring, ideological fundamentalism, has been the curse of humankind for all of our history. It has resulted in the intolerance, the bigotry, the persecution, the violence, the bloodshed and genocide that has been the hallmark of human history. Homo sapiens (Man the Wise) does not seem to live up to his arrogant and self-congratulatory scientific name. We have been slow learners. We have been making the same stupid mistakes in spite of studying our history. While having developed some civilizing attitudes and behaviors, we still engage in the same kinds of intellectual errors we were making over 50,000 years ago.

It took more than 99.99% of our history as a species, but we have finally learned to abandon the religio/subjective mode of thinking to assess and evaluate our relationship with nature, and replace it with the scientific/objective mode of thinking. Our rise above barbarism has not been easy. It has been a long, slow, tortured process of trial and error, all the while making repeated, horrendous mistakes. We are still carrying around the heavy baggage of superstition: magical, mystical thinking and an overpowering desire to find a "School-of-Easy-Answers." The "School-of-Easy-Answers" that some people call "Religion" has not, does not, and cannot provide us with the answers we need in our culture that has evolved in spite of the "anchors" we have been dragging for all of our history.

The Renaissance and the Enlightenment that enabled us to at least partially escape from 1000 years of intellectual stagnation and regression of religio/subjective thought will have to be regenerated and sustained for Western Civilization to achieve the glory that began as a glimmer in Greece ca. 2500 years ago.

There is still hope. If we can intelligently and scientifically direct the evolution of Homo sapiens, (Man-the-not-so-wise) into "Homo intelligenticus," we have a chance at survival beyond the foreseeable future. If not, extinction looms on the horizon.

"In their struggle for the ethical good, teachers of religion must have the stature to give up the doctrine of a personal God, that is, give up that source of fear and hope which in the past placed such vast power in the hands of priests. In their labors they will have to avail themselves of those forces which are capable of cultivating the Good, the True, and the Beautiful in humanity itself. This is, to be sure a more difficult but an incomparably more worthy task . . . ."
—Albert Einstein, "Science, Philosophy and Religion, A Symposium," published by the Conference on Science, Philosophy and Religion in their Relation to the Democratic Way of Life, Inc., New York, 1941). D. 1955.

~~~~~~~~~~~~~~~~~~

I cannot imagine a God who rewards and punishes the objects of his creation, whose purposes are modeled after our own—a God, in short, who is but a reflection of human frailty. Neither can I believe that the individual survives the death of his body, although feeble souls harbor such thoughts through fear or ridiculous egotism. It is enough for me to contemplate the mystery of conscious life perpetuating itself through all eternity, to reflect upon the marvelous structure of the universe which we can dimly perceive, and to try humbly to comprehend even an infinitesimal part of the intelligence manifested in nature.
—Albert Einstein, column for The New York Times, Nov. 9, 1930

Twelve Reasons Why I Reject Christianity

Gods, devils, angels, heaven, and hell are all products of human imagination and exist only in the minds of those who choose to believe in such nonsense. They are the products of primitive, barbaric minds from cultural savages and have no justification in the minds of educated people. They are fictive concepts created by myth makers to further their theological objectives of controlling the minds of credulous, ignorant people. Such ideas are not worthy of my attention, much less my consideration.

Archaic dogmas carried to us from Iron Age cultures are not appropriate for us in our culture and in our time. Any religion must evolve apace within a culture to remain relevant and viable. To suggest that ancient religious myths and legends are the word of a deity is ludicrous and indefensible. With our modern knowledge base we are better equipped and prepared to compose our own moral and ethical codes than any ancient culture.

A religion based on a religious text that sanctions slavery, the physical beating of children, the debasement of women as property and as second class people, keeping concubines (sex slaves), and capital punishment for disobedience, is not a religion for me.

The religious promise of life everlasting in the company of a deity and loved ones who have preceded one in death, in a place of eternal beauty and peace, and sheltered from the vicissitudes of an earthly existence is the cruelest hoax ever perpetrated on human beings. I cannot find solace in lies. I am a product of the evolution of life on earth. I have a finite life span like every other organism, and I accept my mortality as a reality of living. Surviving one's death in any form or fashion is childish, wishful thinking.

A religion that denigrates and demeans women and casts them into second class citizenship, such as nuns, I find repugnant and must be rejected as unwarranted gender hierarchy—blatant sexism.

A religion that preaches a message of fear, guilt, shame, sin, and death can only demean and denigrate people. This is inconsistent with a message of love and compassion. People must love themselves before they can love others. Positive exuberance for a style of life governance has much more appeal for me.

A religion that demeans and denigrates human knowledge retards the growth and development of human culture. I find this deplorable. Our culture grows only in proportion to our cumulative knowledge.

A religion that threatens eternal pain and suffering if strict obedience to priestly mandates is violated is authoritarian, undemocratic, barbaric, and cruel.

The alleged miracles of the Christian scheme of things that were written and included in the canon to justify and supposedly strengthen the veracity of claims or assertions in an age of credulity and superstition are blatant lies today. Falsehoods labeled as truth in a sacred text keep us from realizing our potential as human beings. All Biblical miracles are a denial of and contradictory to the known laws of the universe. Such nonsensical stories are an insult to the intelligence of educated people and have no place in modern culture. They are carried over to us by a priesthood from an age of ignorance.

To accept a religion like Christianity that is based on the Bible which is riddled with contradictions and inconsistencies; smudgy semantic stratagems; obfuscatory passages; literary tricks; muddled chronologies; errors of fact; poorly or misunderstood metaphors, allegories, and symbols; and archaic ideas that are entirely at odds with contemporary community standards would be unmitigated foolishness that insults my intelligence.

In light of the magnitude of human suffering, it is clear that the alleged omni-benevolent god of the Judeo-Christian tradition is impotent to do anything about it, is incompetent to do anything about it, or is totally indifferent to our plight.

To consider that our sun, a minor star, the earth and all of the sister planets could disappear in a puff of dust that would not make a ripple of any real consequence in our galaxy, the Milky Way, which has about a hundred billion stars, much less the cosmos, and to suggest that an imaginary deity of a wandering tribe of pastoral Hebrews of circa 3000 years ago is the creator of the cosmos is the most intellectually indefensible, and at the same time the most arrogant idea ever advanced by a human mind. Only the most ignorant, naive, and credulous mind could ever consider as legitimate such a preposterous idea.

Religious beliefs, even if irrational, have been, and may still be, adaptive in an evolutionary context. They are the glue that holds a community (tribe) together. The commonality of religious beliefs has been a prime factor in making possible the social cohesion necessary for survival. Without this social bonding it is unlikely that Homo sapiens could have survived the vicissitudes of living on this planet.

While religious beliefs have been adaptive for a primitive, insular tribe because it is a necessary factor for cohesiveness, they are divisive in a modern context in which so many people live in such close proximity. Our seemingly natural propensity for xenophobic behavior is exacerbated by religious beliefs that isolate us from others. Tolerance of, and compassion for, others is literally a behavior that is at odds with our evolutionary history.

We still have a difficult time managing our lives with our genetic heritage. Compounding and exacerbating our problems while we persist in adhering to ancient, archaic ideas borne of ignorance of all we have learned as a species in the last 2000 years Is counter productive and unrewarding. Our modern, secular, scientific society is infinitely better equipped and prepared to compose a moral and ethical code as a paradigm for life governance than anything from any source many centuries ago.

Christianity is unacceptable as a source of life governance because it is riddled with incongruities, inconsistencies, contradictions and absurdities. It is hopelessly trapped in a rigid, first century mindset, mired in ancient, archaic concepts, and consequently obsolete for people in the 21st century.

Christian beliefs fly in the face of our modern, scientific understanding of ourselves and the cosmos. Conceived in ignorance, born in superstition, raised in subjective certitude, devoid of any identity with modern reality, Christianity is clearly on the wrong side of history. Sooner or later it is destined for the philosophical trash bin of the consciousness of educated people.

All things considered, and taking the long, broad view of things, Christianity as a focal point in my life is no longer worth my consideration.

We can do better. We have to do better.

Being an atheist is a matter not of moral choice, but of human obligation.

—John Fowles, quoted in
The New York Times Book Review,
May 31, 1998

~~~~~~~~~~~~~~~~~~

. . . I've come to realize it's time to sound the alarm. Whether we brights are a minority or, as I am inclined to believe, a silent majority, our deepest convictions are increasingly dismissed, belittled and condemned by those in power—by politicians who go out of their way to invoke God and to stand, self-righteously preening, on what they call 'the side of the angels.'

. . . Politicians don't think they even have to pay us lip service, and leaders who wouldn't be caught dead making religious or ethnic slurs don't hesitate to disparage the 'godless' among us.

From the White House down, bright-bashing is seen as a low-risk vote getter. And, of course, the assault isn't only rhetorical: the Bush administration has advocated changes in government rules and policies to increase the role of religious organizations in daily life, a serious subversion of the Constitution. It is time to halt this erosion and to take a stand: the United States is not a religious state, it is a secular state that tolerates all religions and—yes—all manner of non religious ethical beliefs as well.

—Daniel C. Dennett, "The Bright Stuff,"
The New York Times, July 12, 2003

Finding Truth in Our Lives

This is a story with three scenarios. The first is a convention of scientists who are presenting their papers that are the fruit of their research—an assertion of a newly discovered truth about some aspect of natural phenomena.

A researcher stands in front of a large group of his peers who are all quite skeptical of assertions from any source. The researcher presents an oral report, nearly always with some visuals that represent the hypothesis, the methodology, the data, and the conclusions of the research. The professional reputation of the researcher lies in the thoroughness, the precision, the accuracy and the efficacy of the research. Questions are asked, flaws are laid bare, and conclusions are challenged. The scrutiny of the research is rigorous and can be grueling. Sloppy methods are condemned, data scrutinized, and the results examined in great detail. A jury of one's professional peers who are highly educated and experienced can be very demanding. A compelling argument based on well-grounded data is an absolute requirement. Unconfirmed or unverifiable data and faith-based arguments are regarded as cognitively worthless.

The scientific process at one and the same time tries to both confirm and deny the legitimacy of assertions from research. This makes the scientific approach to the search for truth about natural phenomena self correcting. While subjective intuition and leaps of imagination play a significant part in the human creative process of scientific research; objective, quantified confirmation is always a necessary part of the establishment of scientific truth.

In the history of humankind and the various means of establishing truth in our lives, the scientific method has produced the most dependable and most reliable truths about natural phenomena ever developed by human ingenuity.

The second scenario is a criminal court of law in which guilt must be established beyond a shadow of a doubt, otherwise the defendant is presumed innocent in our system of jurisprudence. Understandably, a district attorney—the prosecutor in the case before the court—is loathe to bring an indictment against the accused unless he or she can present compelling evidence and a strong argument for the prosecution. Bringing a defendant to trial without this strong ammunition would result in not only losing the case to the defense, but it could be a serious professional embarrassment as well. Again, faith based arguments are without merit. The professional reputation and competency of the prosecutors hang in the balance.

In a court of law the amount and kind of evidence along with rebutted testimony and compelling arguments, that sift and winnow the grain from the chaff, determine the truth upon which guilt or innocence is determined. The process is imperfect, but if competently adjudicated, it is the most reliable means of arriving at objective legal truths.

The third scenario is in a church—a Sunday school. The children who are the objects of the instruction are very vulnerable and prone to regarding their teachers as authority figures. They are very much at risk. The question is: Will they be educated or indoctrinated?

Nearly everyone will accept the idea that true education gives serious attention to the equal presentation of competing and contrasting ideas. The presentation of ideas or stories that are slanted or present only one side of an argument are indoctrination, not true education.

The presentation of ideas or stories that cannot be verified or confirmed in science or in a court of law are regarded as hearsay, and consequently are judged to be cognitively worthless. Such presentations are labeled as propaganda and their worth as reliable information for guidance in one's life is nil.

Ideas or stories given to children as the truth when they are in direct contradiction to the known laws of the universe corrupt their cognitive processing skills. Children are caught in an intellectual trap of cognitive dissonance between the purely subjective/intuitive ideas taught to them as truth in their religion, and the objective/quantifiable truths about natural phenomena of our modern science. Children are caught on the horns of a dilemma: should they believe ancient, obsolete, unverifiable, subjective ideas about natural phenomena borne of fear, ignorance and superstition, or should they accept as true the objective, verifiable explanations of modern science about those same phenomena?

2000 years ago theological explanations for natural phenomena directed towards illiterate masses may have been effective for advancing a religious agenda. Today, in the light of modern science, for educated people, they are not only false, they are lies. Religious stories cannot and must not prevail in a modern context as explanations about the physical and the factual.

Corrupting the minds of children with cognitive dissonance about natural phenomena is child abuse, and should be labeled as criminal behavior. Instead of teaching our children that the Biblical miracles, e.g. virgin births, bodily resurrections of the dead, et. al., are mystical, mythological, allegorical narratives like the mythologies of the Greeks, the Egyptians, the Sumerians, the Romans, the Persians and others, Christians for centuries have indoctrinated their children with the ideas that these myths are historically valid truths.

Clearly, teaching children that they can find truth in their lives about natural phenomena from religious sources is not only doomed to failure, it is misleading, confusing and ultimately destructive.

Raised in the purely subjective culture of religious explanations for at least the first ten years of their life, it is not difficult to understand why Johnny and Jane intuitively eschew the cognitive dissonance of scientific explanations that are in contradiction to the indelible impressions of their early childhood indoctrination.

What has historically been regarded as "Religious Truths" that are not only inconsistent with, but contradictory to, a modern knowledge base must be abandoned in favor of scientifically sound explanations. Children should not have to cope with the cognitive dissonance of contradictory explanations of natural phenomena from ancient religion and from modern science.

If we are going to help our children find truth in their lives in our modern, scientific culture, we will have to assure that they are educated with an accurate, modern knowledge base and not indoctrinated with archaic religious myths taught as historical facts.

The trouble with the world is that the stupid are cocksure and the intelligent are full of doubt.

—Bertrand Russell

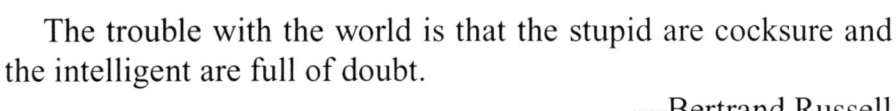

The deeper our insight into the methods of nature . . . the more incredible the popular Christianity seems to us.

—John Burroughs, The Light of Day, 1900

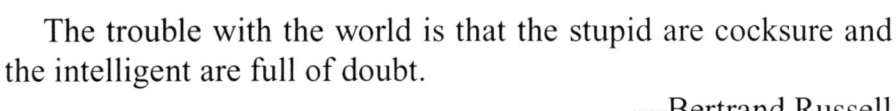

All religions have this in common, that they are an outrage to common sense, for they are pieced together out of a variety of elements some of which seem unworthy, sordid and at odds with man's reason that any strong and vigorous intelligence laughs at them.

—Pierre Charron, Catholic theologian 1541-1603

Getting Up to Speed in the Twenty First Century

The Necessary Intellectual Imperative for the New Millennium

We all have a difficult time keeping up with our rapidly growing and changing culture. Our expanding knowledge base gets deeper and wider every day by quantum leaps. We are reminded of Alice and the Red Queen in Lewis Carroll's, "Through the Looking Glass." The faster they ran the more it seemed they stayed in the same place.

The mass media do a reasonable job keeping us abreast of social and political changes, but they are mediocre at best in helping people to keep apace of the scientific/technological advances that are taking place at an exponential rate. Our knowledge of the physical and the factual has increased so much in the last hundred years that most people are in culture shock. Still, it behooves us to collectively increase our awareness of these giant cultural leaps forward if only to be able to intelligently cast a ballot and be well informed consumers.

An electorate of scientifically illiterate people is more of a handicap than an asset. Our state legislatures do not require scientific literacy for high school graduation, and many college graduates have little more scientific literacy when they graduate than when they matriculated. We are guilty of an egregious error of omission. The costs we are paying for our ignorance are more than we can afford. Given our present attitudes and practices, it is likely to get worse before we can rectify our negligence and make it better.

In order to come to grips with the reality and demands of the 21st century, we find it increasingly necessary to bring our thinking and our behavior up to speed. In order for this to take place, some old and comfortable ideas that have become obsolete will have to be abandoned. Newer ideas from our expanding knowledge base must have a broad understanding and acceptance across all of society. This will require profound changes in educational theory and practice. In the competitive world marketplace of ideas, a higher level of awareness of the new realities has become a prime requisite for maintaining a position of hegemony in the community of nations. Archaic ideas about what is true about natural phenomena derived from subjective religious certitude and borne of the ignorance, magic and superstition of an ancient world view must be replaced by a modern assessment of reality derived from reason, scientifically verifiable evidence, logical inference, and modern, higher order thinking skills.

Specifically, the following ideas will have to be incorporated into the mind set of the public through a massive and revolutionary educational effort. Expect to pay for it. We neglect this intellectual imperative at our peril.

The churches must recognize that their presumed primacy of authority on matters of the physical and the factual in our lives and the cosmos has been superseded and rendered invalid by the advances of science. The churches must take an active (not passive) role in advancing this idea. Historically, the churches with their archaic world view have steadfastly resisted and obstructed the growth and development of Western Civilization by condemning as "worldly" the discoveries of science. All authority about the measurable and the quantifiable in the advance of our culture is in the realm of science. Religion must accommodate and advocate this position.

Biblical "miracles" that deny and defy the known laws of the universe have historically been ideas that could be "sold" to ignorant and credulous people. Today, in view of our modern scientific knowledge base, these assertions are not only false, they are lies. They have no legitimate part in the education of the public at any level. Educating children to be competent, critical thinkers who can employ higher order thinking skills and be adept as problem solvers in the 21st century is a difficult job as it is, without having to first retrofit their brains from the indoctrination of irrationalities they received for years from their church. Religious indoctrination corrupts the cognitive processes of children.

Teaching children that they can find answers about the physical and the factual of natural phenomena (objective truths) from a subjectively derived religious text is doomed to failure and is a gross injustice to the child. True education is the in-depth examination of competing and contrasting ideas. The channeled and shallow mindedness of religious indoctrination is the antithesis of legitimate education. Hungry truth seekers starve to death on a diet of the religio/subjective world view promulgated for centuries by a church committed to the control of the minds of the people whom they should have educated. Religious indoctrination will be an impediment to the intellectual growth and humanizing process of children as long as it persists. Child abuse comes to mind.

Organic evolution is a fact as much as the fact of gravity. The scientific findings of the last 150 years have established the intellectual legitimacy of this great leap forward in the understanding of the changes that have occurred in the approximately three-and-a-half billion-year history of life on earth. The confirming evidence supporting this scientific principle, from many disparate disciplines, is so large, so compelling, and so persuasive that to not give provisional assent is to be stupidly perverse and intractably ignorant. The open-ended nature of scientific truth seeking dictates that there is no final comprehensive understanding of this natural phenomenon. Hence, the search for more knowledge about the evolutionary process will not reach an end point.

People of the religious community who deny the validity of the knowledge of organic evolution do so for ideological reasons that are outside of the purview of science. Their criticisms couched in the language of "Creation science" and "Intelligent Design" have no scientific foundation and are therefore fraudulent and without scientific merit. Legitimate criticism of scientifically-grounded organic evolution can come only from competent science. An avenue of religious subjectivity can never lead to an evaluation of the merits of objective science.

The illogical and irrational ravings of fundamentalists who are determined to discredit science in general, and biological evolution in particular, in an attempt to protect and preserve their archaic and obsolete world view, serve only to obstruct the inevitable march of civilization toward a higher understanding of natural phenomena. Today, fundamentalists of any persuasion are an embarrassment to educated people of all persuasions. The intellectual legitimacy of organic evolution grows every day with our expanding knowledge base. The "Fundamentalists" need to get a grip on life, based on objective reality—something that thus far they have failed to grasp. Calvin, the six-year-old boy of the "Calvin and Hobbes" comic strip once said, "Isn't it sad that some people's grip on their lives is so precarious that they'll embrace any preposterous delusion rather than face an occasional bleak truth."

The concept of a theistic "God" or gods is as old as consciousness. This is probably the most convenient and comfortable concept ever to spring from the imagination of human beings. Benevolent, loving fathers and mothers who will protect us, provide for us, and forgive us, even if they are fictitious, is probably the nicest, warm, fuzzy idea we can create. While it may be comfortable, this barbaric idea no longer has merit for rational, thinking, modern people. Invoking Gods and their attendant theologies is the way ignorant people have explained the natural phenomena that they did not understand. Today, with modern science, we know better than that. We need to acknowledge the new realities of our expanding knowledge base and concurrently abandon those ideas that are shown to be obsolete. This is called cultural evolution.

Creator gods abound in nearly all human cultures, but not one of them has any more veracity than any of the others in spite of the assertions of some people. The many desirable, idealistic human attributes given to gods are clearly archaic, anthropomorphic projections of barbaric, pagan cultures. Such ancient, unwarranted concepts cannot be justified in the thinking or education of modern people.

Today, in our culture, any god must be understood as an archaic myth in the same context as Thor, Zeus, Osiris, Mithra and Marduk. Truly, gods are the measure of our desperation, and theologies are the measure of our gullibility. All of us, especially our children, need to understand that our future is in our hands, and that we cannot expect help from any external source, divine or otherwise. Wishful thinking feels good, but ultimately it is destructive. It is a luxury that intelligent people cannot afford if they are to navigate the hazards of the 21st century.

We know with reasonable certainty that the Old Testament was written by Hebrew priests, their functional analogs, and other religious zealots. The assertion that it was divinely inspired is nothing more than an insupportable assertion by those with a religious agenda who need external support because their premises, assertions and fanciful stories are internally incoherent and cannot prevail under critical scrutiny. The authors of yesteryear were called prophets, but today they are called "Spin Doctors." The reality of both is that they are/were ambitious ideologues who were driven by their consummate egos to bend the will of others to obedience, and to superimpose their agenda on the gullible masses. Invoking divine sanction to support a religio/political agenda has been, and still is, a tool of the exploiters to control and manipulate the exploitees. It has been very successful for many unscrupulous people as they continue to exploit the credulous and the gullible. We should all know better.

We cannot expect to find very many of the answers or solutions for our contemporary problems from an ancient and archaic text. Iron age answers are neither dependable nor reliable for people in a modern scientific/technological culture. Any code of ethics and morals must be composed in the context of contemporary culture and a modern knowledge base. We are better prepared and equipped to do so than anyone in the distant past.

Attitudes and value systems that denigrate or demean human intelligence must be eliminated from any valid world view. Fostering and practicing those ideas that enhance our self esteem are the most rewarding and productive ideas in any instructional curriculum. The focal points of fear, guilt, shame, sin, and death so pervasive in the monotheistic religions must disappear by design. They must be replaced by focal points of confidence, exuberance, pride and the enjoyment of life here and now. Expectations of rewards for the faithful or punishment for evil ones in an ethereal existence beyond death has never been confirmed or verified by anyone. Extending sanction to such a preposterous, barbaric idea, is a cruel and monstrous hoax, and has no place in any instructional program from any authority figure.

All racist and sexist attitudes and practices in all facets of human life must be replaced by egalitarian attitudes and practices. Ancient attitudes and practices derived from archaic, religious, tribal xenophobia and biases were wrong then and are wrong now. Such attitudes and the behaviors derived from them are the most pernicious malignancies in our culture. They are the source of irrational biases fear and prejudice, that result in persecution and bigotry, and that lead to violence.

The concepts of heaven, hell, devils, angels, and their attendant ideas are concepts made by and endorsed by ignorant people. Since such ideas are inconsistent with, and contradictory to, our modern, scientific knowledge base, they are cognitively worthless and consequently have no place in our understanding of either our lives or the cosmos. Such ideas belong in the intellectual trash heap of history and are unworthy of our serious consideration.

The blind, unquestioning, irrational and unjustified religious beliefs, accepted on faith and revelation, that have been an intellectual cancer for all of human history must be abandoned. Blind faith is not only foolishness, it is rank stupidity. In their place, it is in our collective best interests to adopt an approach of skepticism to all claims and assertions until they have undergone the most rigorous scrutiny employing higher order thinking skills of analysis, synthesis and evaluation. Claims and assertions that cannot be supported by compelling evidence and can neither be verified nor confirmed, must be considered as cognitively worthless. We cannot afford to accept or adopt any thesis as truth that violates the known laws of the universe.

We must get our thinking up to speed, and consistent with our times. We must employ our modern knowledge base in order to make reliable decisions. We must be able to assess reality with the newest and best known tools that we have. A realistic evaluation of the newest information that we have must be an ongoing process. We cannot afford to embrace, adopt and defend an archaic, static world view, conceived in the cultural milieu of tribal ignorance, fear, magic and superstition of 2000 years ago as we chart a new course to navigate the hazards of the 21st century.

Others will doubtless add to those changes shown here, but we must start now! We probably won't be able to realize soon all of the things that have been detailed here, but we can provide the impetus and the foundation on which our children can build. We can start now, or our children will start later, and they will wonder why we didn't.

Errors of commission may be forgivable; but errors of omission are not.

Gullibility and credulity are considered undesirable qualities in every department of human life—except religion . . . . Why are we praised by godly men for surrendering our 'godly gift' of reason when we cross their mental thresholds? . . . . Atheism strikes me as morally superior, as well as intellectually superior, to religion. Since it is obviously inconceivable that all religions can be right, the most reasonable conclusion is that they are all wrong.

—Christopher Hitchens, "The Lord and the Intellectuals,"
Harper's (July 1982), cited by James A. Haught in
2,000 Years of Disbelief, 1996.

~~~~~~~~~~~~~~~~~~

If you talk to God, you are praying. If God talks to you, you have schizophrenia.

—Psychiatrist Thomas Szasz, M.D.

~~~~~~~~~~~~~~~~~~

"Religion is the belief in future life and in God. I don't believe in either"

—Clarence Darrow

Logic and Theology:
A Syllogism and Case Study

Most people have heard of syllogisms, and some know what they are. A syllogism is an intellectual construct in logic. A syllogism consists of a major premise, a minor premise and a conclusion. In order for the conclusion to be true, both the major and minor premises must be true. If the conclusion is not true, then either the major or minor premise, or both, must be false.

I offered one of my Christian friends a syllogism for his consideration. The major premise was, "God is perfect." The minor premise was, "God made Man in his own image." I asked my friend if the premises were consistent with his religious conviction. He responded in the affirmative to both premises. I then asked him if a logical conclusion would be, "Therefore, Man is perfect." He could see where I was going and balked, but I persisted and asked if the conclusion was inescapable. He reluctantly agreed, so I proceeded.

I asked if he would accept "Intelligent Designer" or just "Designer" as a synonym for God. He agreed, so I pressed on.

Would an Intelligent Designer :

Put vestigial mammary glands and nipples on a male mammal?

Design humans with only one set of permanent teeth when crocodiles and sharks can replace lost teeth throughout their lives?

Design humans with a spine, that while adapted to upright posture for bipedal locomotion, is far from perfect—as witness the lower back problems so nearly universal among humans and absent in quadrupeds?

Allow design flaws like varicose veins and hemorrhoids and hernias so common among humans that reflect the fact that we have evolved from quadrupeds, albeit imperfectly because these afflictions are unknown in quadrupeds? The hydraulic pressure produced by an upright column of blood in our veins was not adequately accounted for by an "Intelligent Designer" for an upright, bipedal animal.

Design the sinuses in our cheek bones to drain upwards against the force of gravity? The same sinuses drain down with the force of gravity in quadrupeds.

Design the retina in our eyes with a blind spot?

Deny us the ability to regenerate eyes, and arms, and legs, lost by violence or accident since lobsters, crabs and crayfish can do so?

Design a human body with such a massive head connected to a torso with such a frail peduncle that it makes the neck so prone to serious damage?

Design an upright, bipedal animal with knees that are so inadequate to absorb the wrenching forces we put upon them? Quadrupeds don't have the knee problems we have.

Design a woman's body so that giving birth was a life threatening event?

Design a food tube and breathing passage in common so that accidentally choking to death is a distinct possibility?

Design our alimentary canal with a vestigial organ like our useless appendix?

While the evolutionary process produces genetic variations by chance, it favors and conserves preferentially by natural selection those variations that work, not necessarily those variations that would be deemed perfect. The many "design flaws" in the human body are inconsistent with an omniscient, Intelligent Designer.

My friend has an academic background in human genetics and is acutely aware of the hundreds of documented genetic defects in humans, with more being documented every day. He acknowledged all these design "errors" and agreed that, yes, an omniscient

"Intelligent Designer" would not have made such egregious errors.

I then asked if we could return to our syllogism. I reminded him that in the logical construct of the syllogism if the conclusion is false, then either the major premise or minor premise, or both, must be false. Since humans are inarguably not perfect, and riddled with "design" flaws, which premise would he declare false first?

Suddenly, he seemed like he had been stripped of one of his most cherished illusions. His spine stiffened, however, and he retreated into denial in order to cope with the uncomfortable reality he had just encountered. I can present this line of thinking to him without him taking offense at me personally. This is why I value him as a friend, and we continue to be friends in spite of the fact that our world views are diametrically opposed. I would not present this argument to most other friends or acquaintances because faced with the inescapable conclusion of the logic in the syllogism they would likely take extreme umbrage because I had punctured one of their favorite balloons.

My friend finds convenience and solace in his religion. It is difficult to fault people for that since they are victims of the indoctrination they received as children, and they still cling to that security blanket. People will continue to cling to religious answers to their questions about natural phenomena in spite of the fact that they are illogical, irrational, intellectually indefensible, and fly in the face of critical thinking. The logical, rational and intellectually defensible answers of science to our questions about natural phenomena have been subordinated to a religious, God at any price ideology.

The natural world abounds with chaos and unpredictability. The constancy, predictability, and certitude provided by revealed religions is easy and convenient. It makes the lives of the believers easier, simpler and more comfortable. The tragedy of this kind of belief lies in the fact that people continue to cling to irrational beliefs in spite of allegedly achieving higher levels of education and experience. They place comfort before logic, convenience before rationality, and faith before reason. While emotions are undeniably a very important part of our psyche and persona, allowing our emotions a higher priority than our intellect will preclude the realization of our potential as human beings.

There are costs when we believe in falsehoods. Believing in falsehoods corrupts our cognitive processes, it precludes a wise management of our lives and our resources, it interferes with our relationship with others, it destroys our credibility in the eyes of knowledgeable people, and it is the biggest bug-a-boo when it comes to making public policy. The costs are too high if even at the level of the individual believer, but ultimately the costs to society at large, for the comfort received, are prohibitively expensive.

The Christian religion not only was at first attended with miracles, but even at this day cannot be believed by any reasonable person without one.

—David Hume, "An Enquiry Concerning Human Understanding," 1748

~~~~~~~~~~~~~~~~~

Religion has been compelled by science to give up one after another of its dogmas, of those assumed cognitions which it could not substantiate.

—Herbert Spencer, "First Principles," 1862

~~~~~~~~~~~~~~~~~

"Wandering in a vast forest at night, I have only a faint light to guide me. A stranger appears and says to me: 'My friend, you should blow out your candle in order to find your way more clearly.' This stranger is a theologian."

—Denis Diderot

Mr. Townsend, Faith and Truth

Shortly before I was to enter eighth grade I was in conversation with some friends who were a year older than I was. They were telling me about Mr. Townsend, the eighth grade science teacher. They were telling me that he was strict and mean, even harsh and demanding. My friends didn't like him and they painted a picture of Mr. Townsend that colored my mind in a negative way. I didn't like it at all. I was very interested in science; I had done well in seventh grade and wanted to do well in eighth grade science which would be starting shortly. I brooded on my friend's views until I entered Mr. Townsend's class.

I wasn't doing well for the first three or four weeks. My grades were quite below what I had wanted and expected. I had an attitude problem derived from the views of others. It did occur to me, though, that I didn't see Mr. Townsend like my friends had described him. He was demanding, even tough, but he was an excellent teacher and fair. I found myself liking him. I remembered what my friends had said about Mr. Townsend. It occurred to me that I had let them do my thinking for me.

I went to see Mr. Townsend after school. We must have talked for 30 minutes or so. It all went very well. I found out that I not only liked him—I admired him. I was a straight "A" student in his class the rest of the year.

I thought a lot about that whole experience and learned what may be one of the most important lessons anyone can ever learn. I learned that accepting someone else's word about what was true based on faith can be very hazardous. I had faith in my friends, but they had offered no evidence to support their assertions about Mr. Townsend. All they offered was unsupported testimony—a personal anecdotal narrative. Nothing about Mr. Townsend had been either verified or confirmed. I had been victimized by my own faith. I learned the value and importance of skepticism, but I was still an imperfect and immature learner.

I carried this lesson with me, but as an adolescent I was still in the habit of accepting the views of authority figures as the truth, as I think we all were at that time in our lives. I was impressionable and naive. I tried to believe, but it wasn't always easy. I asked a lot of questions. Some of the answers were satisfying, but others were not. Some teachers gave vague, evasive, inconsistent and unconvincing answers. This was especially true in my religious indoctrination that was called education. I was a Christian by default because everyone else was, and it was expected of me.

Sometimes my experience with Mr. Townsend would come back to me. I would remember that I had formed an opinion with insufficient data—inadequate information. I had committed myself to an idea or proposition without examining contrasting arguments from other people—other sources. I had even become defensive about some of my views albeit they were not well grounded—but I had faith that I was right anyway. I hadn't always seen the other side of the coin, much less examined it.

Probably the three most important things that college students learn, or should have learned, by graduation time from a liberal education is: (1) an appreciation for how much there is that they don't know; (2) that certainty and absolutism can be the easiest, but most dangerous things in the world; and (3) giving assent to, or endorsing any idea, proposition, or story from any source that is not supported by compelling evidence leaves one open to exploitation and manipulation by others; that regarding any idea as immune to scrutiny and examination, that cannot be corroborated from some dependable, credible, external source is not only foolhardy, it is stupidity.

Truth by faith and revelation has historically given people license to: believe in and justify the persecution of others of different persuasion; to legislate discrimination against minorities; to preach divisiveness and bigotry; to justify hatred, atrocities murder and genocide. To Adolph Hitler, a committed Catholic, faith and belief was his highest priority.

Truth by faith is surely the easiest, most convenient and most comfortable way of trying to navigate through the vicissitudes of life. It is also the most hazardous, dangerous, and destructive path we can follow. Truth by faith provides the roots and support for the most heinous of crimes.

It wasn't part of Mr. Townsend's curriculum or lesson plan, and probably not his intent, but I learned some of life's most important lessons in his class: keep an open mind, being receptive to new ideas doesn't mean I have to adopt them for my own, regard all claims and assertions by others with a healthy degree of skepticism, examine competing and contrasting ideas carefully, delay judgment until I have as much relevant information as possible, regard all truths as tentative and provisional, be prepared to adopt new knowledge when the evidence strongly suggests that I should, be prepared to abandon positions or views that have proven to be obsolete or irrelevant, and regard all unsupported, irrefutable, unverifiable claims and assertions as cognitively worthless. If you are a sheep and need a shepherd, by all means let someone else do your thinking for you, or you are likely to make grievous, maybe fatal mistakes. However, if you are reasonably intelligent and educable, make sure that you have acquired an adequate knowledge base, learn to use higher order thinking skills, and learn to think for yourself. If you don't, or can't, rest assured someone else will tell you what to think, how you should think, and what you should, even must, believe!

Then you will voluntarily pay a heavy price for this service.

No one will promise you that realizing your potential as a thinking human being will be easy.

There are no gods, no devils, no angels, no heaven or hell. There is only our natural world. Religion is but myth and superstition that hardens hearts and enslaves minds.

—Anne Nicol Gaylor,

~~~~~~~~~~~~~~~~~~

If some good evidence for life after death were announced, I'd be eager to examine it; but it would have to be real scientific data, not mere anecdote. As with the face on Mars and alien abductions, better the hard truth, I say, than the comforting fantasy. And in the final tolling it often turns out that the facts are more comforting than the fantasy.

—Carl Sagan, "The Fine Art of Baloney Detection,"
from The Demon-Haunted World:
Science As A Candle In The Dark, 1996

~~~~~~~~~~~~~~~~~~

Gods exist only in ignorance of the laws of the universe. When people are appropriately educated they have no need of fanciful superstitious imaginings and subjective or conjectural speculations to explain themselves, their world or the cosmos. The magical thinking of organized religions is a paradigm that can only lead to an intellectual Black Hole.

—L. Rodney Sheffer

My God Exists!

A friend of mine told me that he loves, honors, worships and obeys his god.

I said, "That's nice—can you detect your god with any of your senses?"

He replied, "No, but I know he exists anyway."

I said, "We have been taught that all human knowledge comes to us through our senses, and only through our senses, and I don't know of any exceptions to that."

"But, I still know my god exists." he replied.

I said, "Do you mean you believe your god exists or do you know your god exists?"

"I know my god exists!" he said.

"Keep in mind, I replied, that whatever one knows to be true can be demonstrated to be true, otherwise, what you hold to be true can only be understood to be beliefs. How can you justify saying that you know your god exists? What evidence can you offer me to warrant the belief that your god exists?"

"I don't need any evidence that my god exists—the Bible says god exists—that's all the evidence I need." he said.

"The Bible cannot be regarded as evidence that your god exists." I replied.

"Why not?" he asked?"

I said, "The Bible is just a book—it is not evidence of anything, but a book."

He said, "But the Bible is the word of God."

"How do you know that?" I replied.

"My priest said so." he said.

"Then you think that the Bible is the word of your god because your priest taught you so." I said.

He said, "Yes."

"What if your priest was wrong?" I said.

He said, "My priest wouldn't lie to me!"

I said, "I didn't say he lied to you—I asked, "What if he were wrong?"

"I have faith that he is right." He said.

I replied, "Let's see if I have this right. You believe that your God exists, but you cannot supply any evidence to support that assertion, and you believe that the Bible is the word of your God because your priest says so. This is what you have been taught."

"That is correct." he said.

I said, "Do the words gullible and credulous mean anything to you?"

"Yeah, I know what they mean." He said.

I asked, "How well do you know your Bible?"

"I have read parts of it," he said.

"I suppose you have read only the parts that your priest asked you to read—is that so?" I said.

"Mostly that is true." He said.

I said, "Since you believe that your God inspired the whole Bible—indirectly authored the whole book, you would expect it to be consistent in its content and message, devoid of contradiction, factually correct and error free."

"Absolutely!" he said.

"What would you say if I told you that the Bible was loaded with inconsistencies, contradictions, factual errors, interpolations, redactions, copyists errors and fiction and forgery as well?"

He said, "I would say you were wrong—you'd have to be wrong— the Bible is the word of God, and he is never wrong."

I replied. "The best Biblical scholars in the world, people who have devoted their life to the critical study of the Bible, those who know the most about the Bible, agree that this is all true."

He said, "I would have a hard time believing that."

"I'm sure of that." I said.

"If what you say is true, then my priest has to be wrong." He said.

"Now you're getting it! I said.

"I still don't believe it! he said.

"Why not? I inquired.

"I still have my faith." He said.

"Does that mean that you are basing your faith on faith"? I asked.

"I guess so." He said.

"Believing is easy isn't it? I asked.

"Yeah, I guess so—I don't like to have to think about it much." He replied.

I said, "That explains a lot of things."

The human mind is greater than any book. The mind sits in judgment on every book. If there be truth in the book, we take it; if error, we discard it. Why refer this to the Bible? In this country, the Bible has been used to support slavery and capital punishment; while in the old countries, it has been quoted to sustain all manner of tyranny and persecution. All reforms are anti-Bible.

> —William Lloyd Garrison, remarks at the 5th national woman's rights conference in Philadelphia on Oct. 18, 1854. History of Woman Suffrage,

~~~~~~~~~~~~~~~~~~

I have no faith in the sense of comforting beliefs which persuade me that all my troubles are blessings in disguise . . . . Creeds pretend to explain the total universe in terms comprehensible to the human intellect, and that pretension seems to me bound to be invalid . . . .

The belief that all higher life is governed by the idea of renunciation poisons our moral life . . . . If we do not live for pleasure we will soon find ourselves living for pain . . .

> —Rebecca West, cited by Warren Allen Smith in Who's Who in Hell

The Objective and the Subjective:
Two Domains of Thinking

Philosophy means different things to different people, but essentially the role of philosophy for the public is to provide a kind of superior thinking that is above that of the rank and file. Philosophy is an attempt to correct errors in thought. The better minds in a culture provide a deeper and broader thinking than that found on the street.

Different ideas advanced by different philosophers have met with different degrees of acceptance over the centuries; some ideas have persisted and have had a profound and lasting influence in human experience and some have perished. Since human culture is cumulative, this is not surprising.

I have read and studied the philosophical ideas of scores of philosophers and have not found one that so impressed me that I would want to be a disciple of any particular philosopher. While I was inclined to agree in part with a number of philosophers, it turns out that all of them were wrong about something or other. This is probably inevitable because even philosophers make judgments based on what is known in their time. No one can make judgments on what is unknown. Cultures are cumulative and inevitably they evolve through time; consequently philosophies evolve as well.

While Socrates, Plato, Aristotle, Democritus, Lucretius, Seneca, Kant, Hume, Nietzsche and a long list of others were very influential, none of them were right about everything they had to say about reality.

Certainly, one of the most common intellectual errors made by people is that they confuse or misuse the domain of the objective and quantitative with the domain of the subjective and qualitative.

This seems to have been a common phenomenon for all of known history.

The objective/quantitative domain of thought includes all of the physical and the factual things that we must consider in our deliberations. Any natural phenomenon that can be observed, measured and quantified is in the realm of what we now call science and must be addressed with intellectual objectivity. Certainly, the best science that uses great leaps of imagination and intuition in the creative process are subjective, but all of the truths of science must be verifiable and objectified for validity. Hunches and feelings play a part in human conceptions, but they cannot be quantified and therefore cannot be used as a part of objective truth.

The subjective/qualitative domain includes abstractions like art, love, music, imagination, intuition, truth, ethics, and morality. These things are of profound importance in our lives, but attempting to quantify things that have such a huge element of emotion leads invariably into an irresolvable quagmire. They are best assessed and evaluated by nonobjective means. This isn't always easy, and serious disagreement is to be expected in the process.

Humans have an inherent need to know the truth about things that concern them. The problem often centers on knowing which domain should be used to lead them to reliable answers to their questions. Addressing a problem and attempting to arrive at the most reliable answers while using the wrong domain will inevitably result in a gross misunderstanding or misinterpretation of reality.

The growth and development of Western Civilization required that both domains be employed in an appropriate manner. Neither domain can be employed as the sole means of assessing reality. The problem that was largely responsible for the depth and duration of the Dark Ages, a thousand years of intellectual regression and stagnation, was that the Catholic Church, in a position of absolute authority, rarely if ever employed the objective/quantitative domain in its attempts to assess reality. The Catholic Church, with its roots in ancient Hebrew culture, was locked almost entirely in the subjective/ qualitative domain. The scientific, objective/quantitative domain was not in the tool kit of the church. Consequently, there was a predictable misinterpretation and misunderstanding of natural phenomena. Now we can only make informed speculation about where Western Civilization would be in its growth and development if the Roman Emperor Constantine would have had the wisdom to insist on the separation of church and state. Alas, he made the most egregious error of governance in the history of Western Civilization by merging the power and influence of church and state. Objectivity and quantification were emasculated and subordinated to the nearly exclusive subjectivity of ecclesiastical thinking. Cultural development stagnated for 1000 years. We are still the poorer for this catastrophic intellectual error.

The Renaissance was an awakening and rebirth of the human spirit that succeeded in spite of the intellectual stranglehold that the Church had maintained for ten centuries, not because of it. Objectivity and quantification became a major part of the thinking of the cognoscenti of Europe and resulted in an explosion of knowledge and culture. The giant intellectual leap forward of the Renaissance was predicated on an objective/ quantitative means of assessing and evaluating natural phenomena. In spite of the Renaissance, the Reformation, and the Enlightenment, much of the confusion of subjectivity with objectivity still adversely affects our epistemology and cognitive processing.

For more than 150 years the need for making a sharp distinction between objective and subjective thinking has made possible the development of our science, our technology and our culture. Still, this confusion over which domain to use remains with us like a chronic disease. The expectations and insistence of the religious community to provide us with answers to our questions about natural phenomena is what precipitated and perpetuated the intellectual stagnation of 1000 years of the Dark Ages when superstition and magic held sway and power over the minds of nearly everyone.

The correct answers to our questions about the physical and the factual have always been in the realm of science—the objective/ quantitative domain. We have to break the stranglehold and obfuscation of ecclesiastical thinking when we need answers to our questions about natural phenomena. We could continue our growth and development in an unfettered way if the leaders in our Executive, Legislative, and Judicial branches of government clearly recognized the need and utility of the separate uses of the objective/ quantitative domain from the subjective/qualitative domain in their decision-making process. Alas, the intellectual sophistication of our leaders, like that of our electorate, has not kept pace with the advance of our scientific culture. We cannot afford to have scientifically illiterate governing bodies in a position to formulate public policy, but we do.

It is difficult and perhaps unreasonable to expect that legislators who are a product of our educational policies of the past create and mandate changes that would be outside the realm of their own experience. Clearly, however, this is what is needed.

The electorate, from which a democratic leadership has been distilled, is still laboring under the illusion that reliable answers to our questions about natural phenomena can be found in an ancient, archaic, and obsolete text that is wired in the first century of the Common Era. The futility of this approach to finding answers to our questions about natural phenomena would seem obvious to all. Somehow, this has escaped too many of us. This has been and continues to be a cultural and societal disaster.

Ninety-nine percent of what we have learned from science about ourselves, our world, and the cosmos has been learned in the last century—in the lifetimes of people who are alive today. The culture shock produced by this quantum leap in our knowledge base is more than most people have been able to understand. It is obvious that we need to redouble our effort and our expenditures on education.

None of us, either individually or collectively, can give sanction to a claim from religions of any kind that they have primacy of authority about questions or answers about the physical or the factual. Long ago we passed the point in our history when we could live with the intellectual errors inherent in that kind of thinking. The common thread in the fabric of all educational curricula should make clear the distinction between the two domains of thinking.

People should not expect their religion to provide them with any answers that are addressed by any of the sciences. Natural phenomena of any kind, biological, astronomical, geological or evolutionary are exclusively in the physical and factual realm of objective/quantitative thinking. This may be a revolutionary change in thinking for some people, but they will either have to make the necessary changes or face intellectual extinction because they are on the wrong side of history, and the wrong side of philosophy.

Free thought means fearless thought. It is not deterred by legal penalties, nor by spiritual consequences. Dissent from the Bible does not alarm the true investigator, who takes truth for authority not authority for truth. The thinker who is really free, is independent; he is under no dread; he yields to no menace; he is not dismayed by law, nor custom, nor pulpits, nor society—whose opinion appeals so many. He who has the manly passion of free thought, has no fear of anything, save the fear of error.

—George Jacob Holyoake, The Origin and Nature of Secularism, Ch. 3 (1896)

~~~~~~~~~~~~~~~~~~~

That's all religion is—some principle you believe in . . . man has accomplished far more miracles than the God he invented. What a tragedy it is to invent a God and then suffer to keep him King.

—Rod Steiger, Playboy (July interview, 1969)

Science, Religion and Change

Why do some religionists, especially fundamentalists, react so negatively to science in general and biological evolution in particular? Why are they so determined to undermine and proscribe evolution from biology text books? Why are they so bent on forcing objective, scientifically derived truths about organic evolution into a subjective straitjacket of their religious ideology? Is it because they want to improve the quality of science education in American schools? I don't think so.

Those who take a contrary position to the findings adopted by the world scientific community must see these findings as a threat to their religious ideas. If the findings of modern science are perceived to be in contradiction to religious dogma, then a critical examination of the assertions of both would seem to be well advised. The relative merits of each can be evaluated and an informed choice can be made.

If religions have the intellectual merit that their advocates claim for them, then nothing science has to say about natural phenomena could possibly make any difference since what is true, is what is true. Condemning scientific truths about natural phenomena cannot advance a contrary agenda.

Religionists recognize that if objective, scientific claims of truth about natural phenomena are in contradiction to their subjective, religious ideas of these same phenomena, then their religious ideas collapse like a castle of sand on a beach with an incoming tide. The scientific truths based on compelling evidence, logic, reason and verifiability render religious explanations based on faith and revelation as unworthy of our consideration.

Probably the most difficult thing anyone has to do is to admit that an idea that they have long believed is true is really false, and has been superseded by new knowledge. As the human knowledge base expands, this is inevitable. Adjusting to new realities may be difficult at times, but it is necessary if one is to remain competitive in the world marketplace of ideas in the 21st century.

Not a single idea ever advanced by the world scientific community has ever been supported by as much compelling evidence, logic and reason as the ideas explained by the Neo-Darwinian synthesis on organic evolution. Like the sand castle on the beach, the fiercely willful, archaic ignorance of religious absolutism about natural phenomena is being swept away into oblivion by the rising tide of our expanding, scientific knowledge base.

Has it ever been more true that change is inevitable, but growth is optional?

The greatest contribution nonbelievers have made to the world has been the Constitution of the United States. Consider how very heretical to a religious world was the idea of a Constitution predicated on 'We, the People.'

—Queen Silver, Humanity's Gain from Unbelief

~~~~~~~~~~~~~~~~~~

Religion is the most malevolent of all mind viruses. We should get rid of it as quickly as we can.

—Author Arthur C. Clarke, Popular Science, Aug. 2004

~~~~~~~~~~~~~~~~~~

Creeds are not guide-boards; they are tombstones. On every creed can be read three words: 'Here lies'—and such lies!

—Marilla M. Ricker (1840-1920), Science Against Creeds:
I Am Not Afraid Are You?

Some Questions for Christians

How important are academic honesty and intellectual integrity to you?

Does compromising principle for expediency offend your sense of ethics or morality?

Do you regard yourself as open minded? Are you able to, and have you ever, changed your firmly held opinion or view on an issue because compelling evidence and strong arguments make such a change prudent and advisable?

Does a high level of well informed scholarship matter to you as you evaluate what you will accept as "true?"

What does the expression "Higher Criticism" mean to you?

Do you appreciate and understand the reasons for regarding claims of truth as tentative and provisional?

Are you concerned about the inherent risks of being a part of a 75% majority?

Are you concerned that the doctrines and dogmas of your religion that are locked into so much absolute certainty are dangerous?

Are you concerned that the static nature of your ancient religion will render your world view obsolete in a rapidly evolving modern culture and society?

Does it matter to you that your religion is based on and derived from the views and values of an ancient, pastoral, Bronze Age tribal culture?

Does it concern you that nothing of what we have learned about ourselves, the world and the cosmos in the past 2000 years has been incorporated into the belief structure of your religion?

Does it concern you that so many of the old "truths" of Christianity are now regarded in the light of a modern knowledge base as absurdities and impossibilities? See question #1.

Are you aware that many of the assertions of Christianity can neither be proven nor refuted, and are therefore of dubious merit?

Does it concern you that all of the alleged miracles of the Bible are in absolute contradiction to the known laws of the universe?

Are you aware that the Jesus myth has been derived from antecedent pagan Egyptian, Sumerian, Babylonian, Persian, and Canaanite myths and ancient Hebrew expectations of a messiah, and therefore cannot be regarded as divinely inspired?

Are you aware that there is no reliable corroborating evidence for the Jesus myth outside of the Gospels?

How do you reconcile the fact that the hundreds of inconsistencies and contradictions in the Bible totally refute the allegation that the Bible is the word of an omniscient god?

Have you recognized that all of the mystical, mythological, allegorical, narratives of the Greek, Roman, Egyptian, Sumerian, Persian and Babylonian cultures were taught as and understood as myths and NOT as factual history?

Have you asked why all of the stories of the Bible have been taught as factual history when all of the stories of other religions have been taught as and understood as cultural myths?

Wouldn't the alleged Jesus, as an omniscient god, have committed his teachings in writing like other self appointed, self authenticating "messengers?

Does it seem odd to you that no one has any real idea of when the alleged Jesus was born or when he died or any other dates in his life?

Have you been aware that none of the scores of writers and historians of the 1st century wrote anything about the Jesus of the Gospels in spite of the extraordinary events that centered on his alleged life?

Were you aware that every trait, character, feature, and event in the life of the alleged Jesus was a part of the myths of numerous other man/god hero figures in middle eastern mythologies that predated the first century by hundreds, even thousands of years?

Given the biased religious indoctrination you received as an intellectually vulnerable child, have you given an appropriate amount of time, effort and attention to an examination of the evidence and arguments that refute the Christian scheme of things? See #1.

Does it concern you that the entire Christian scheme of things has been derived from ancient, barbaric, pagan concepts?

Are you aware that virtually all religions are founded on a gross misunderstanding and misinterpretation of natural phenomena that are now satisfactorily understood and explained by science?

Has your priest or pastor explained to you that every book in the Bible is riddled with well-documented examples of fiction, fraud and forgery by highly competent Biblical scholars? If not, ask them, why not?

If you have been taught that the Bible is the word of a god, have you asked how you know that is believed to be true?

Given the hundreds of inconsistencies, contradictions, errors of fact, muddled chronologies, and its internal incoherence do you still believe that the Bible is the word of an omniscient deity?

Have you ever in your education learned that claims or assertions that are not, and cannot be, supported by compelling evidence are regarded by educated people to be cognitively worthless?

Are you inclined to believe as true what you have been taught even though it cannot be and has never been verified or confirmed in any way?

Have the hazards of believing based on faith ever been explained to you? Do you understand why this is so dangerous?

Have you ever challenged or even questioned your priest or pastor about the assertions they claimed were the truth? If you have, were the answers you got satisfactory? If not, have you wondered why not?

Do you believe that if an idea is emotionally satisfying that it is intellectually justified and defensible?

With regard to your priest or your pastor or Sunday school teacher, have you ever asked yourself, "What if they are wrong?" Could they be wrong? Might their teachers have been wrong?

Was your religious indoctrination given with a balance of competing and contrasting ideas? Why Not?

What do you think is the difference between education and indoctrination?

How is indoctrination different from "brain washing?"

Were you intellectually vulnerable and impressionable as a child?

In your search for truth do you understand the value and importance of skepticism and critical examination of the claims and assertions of others?

What did Socrates mean when he allegedly said, "The unexamined life is not worth living."

In your experience, has petitionary prayer been effective?

Can you discuss the merits or lack thereof, of your religious beliefs calmly and without becoming anxious, hostile or aggressive?

Why didn't the Judeo/Christian god have a wife or daughters? Was this blatant sexism divinely inspired?

Since Christianity has relatively little to do with the Jesus figure and mostly to do with the views of St. Paul, St. Augustine, and some from St. Thomas Aquinas, why should we care what these ancient religious ideologues had to say about anything?

Many Christians (and even some theologians) in the light of modern knowledge, have come to grips with the idea that a theistic god is no longer a tenable or intellectually defensible idea. In view of our present state of knowledge and comprehension of the Christian scheme of things, how close are you to agreeing with these modern views?

Most Jews believe that they are the chosen people of their god. Do you believe this is true? Why or why not?

Would you put any credibility in anything written if you knew the authors could not be identified?

Is your "God" a fact or myth?

Is your "God" internal or external?

Is "heaven" a place—a location? How about "hell"?

Except for a few, why do we know so little if anything about the Apostles?

If you are not Jewish, why are you worshiping a Jewish god?

Do you understand that using the strictly subjective Bible to explain the objectivity of natural phenomena has resulted in an intellectual and cultural disaster for Western Civilization?

In view of the fact that our culture has, and is, evolving so rapidly, does giving assent to religious dogma and doctrine that hasn't changed in many centuries give you cause for pause?

Does submission to the will of an incomprehensible, unknowable, ineffable, arbitrary authority figure seem dangerous to you?

Are you concerned that none of the monotheistic religions has contributed anything to our knowledge base for many centuries?

Can we afford to have among us authority figures like priests and pastors who are scientifically illiterate, or those who fail to acknowledge the intellectual legitimacy of modern scientific findings?

Since both science and religion are human attempts to understand and explain our relationship with nature, how do you justify choosing one in preference to the other?

What new truths has Christianity given us in the last 2000 years?

What has the badly worn-out pagan myth of a crucified Christ figure contributed to our enlightenment and the development of our civilization?

Can your hypotheses of gods, devils, angels, heaven and hell be tested for their veracity?

If the Jews are/were the "chosen people" of their god, then all of us non-Jews are among the "unchosen." Is this a god for you?

Would an omniscient, omnipotent god expect his "children" to take his existence on faith?

Are we any better informed about the Judeo-Christian god now than people were 2000 years ago?

How much joyful, exuberant laughter has Christianity given us in the last 2 millennia?

Is your god real or imaginary? Keep in mind that "real" things are demonstrably true.

If you were on trial for a crime would you object if the testimony against you was based on someone's subjective religious faith and was devoid of objective evidence?

When I asked a Christian where heaven was he replied, "It is out past Orion!" Do you agree?

If your god is real why is there so much disagreement about what or who, god is even among the theologians who are supposed to have the most comprehensive knowledge of the subject?

If you believe in only one god, how do you explain the Trinity?

Consistent with modern ideas about rigorous truth telling in any intellectual venue, e.g., academic, business, scientific or jurisprudence, how much veracity can we find in the unsupported and unverified allegations or assertions of the Christian scheme of things?

Some scholars have alleged that theology is based on nothing more than subjective speculation and unsupported conjecture; that it has no data; that none of its claims can be verified or confirmed; that no reliable external corroboration has been available; that theology is therefore without any real intellectual merit whatever. Do you agree? Why or why not?

Were those people who wrote the Bible as well equipped and prepared to prescribe and proscribe what we should believe and how we should behave than the better minds among us today?

Would you renounce your intellectual integrity to preserve your dream of heaven?

When one is ignorant about nature one can explain all natural phenomena as an act of a deity. Do we then have a better understanding of Nature?

If the ancient Hebrew cosmology was so weak that they didn't even know that the earth was a sphere, how can we place any credibility in the rest?

If there is only one true god wouldn't we all "know" and understand this god in the same context?

If the more mature, sophisticated, and intellectual people among us are above jealousy, would it not be better to emulate them than a jealous god?

How much doubt do you have about the Christian scheme of things?

Theologians are delusional intellectual speculators trapped in a mental thicket of obfuscation and confusion of their own making all the while destined for intellectual extinction. Should we follow their example?

After thousands of years of worshipping "God", how much closer are we to understanding this vague, nebulous, ineffable, incomprehensible, subjective abstraction?

If you are a Christian, Muslim or Jew and disavow all but one of the thousands of gods listed in our libraries and I disavow all of them, how much different am I than you?

I ask of Christians—As you worship your god, does that give you the right to hate those who do not share your irrational, illogical superstitious beliefs?

Are you telling me that your just, merciful and loving god sends fallible human beings to an eternity of pain and suffering for a "finite" sin?

Since the "soul" is the essence of consciousness, and consciousness is the function of a viable brain, does it not follow that the "soul" becomes an indefensible idea when the brain dies?

It is neither Madonna-worship nor saint-worship, but the evangelical self-worship and hell-worship—gloating, with an imagination as unfounded as it is foul, over the torments of the damned, instead of the glories of the blest,—which have in reality degraded the languid powers of Christianity to their present state of shame and reproach.

—John Ruskin, "Fors Clavigera" (1875)

~~~~~~~~~~~~~~~~~~~

It is chilling to think that the same people who persecuted the wise women and men of Europe, its midwives and healers, then crossed the oceans to Africa and the Americas and tortured and enslaved, raped, impoverished, and eradicated the peaceful, Christlike people they found. And that the blueprint from which they worked, and still work, was the Bible.

—Alice Walker, "The Only Reason You Want to Go to Heaven Is That You Have Been Driven Out of Your Mind."

The Fatal Flaw in the Thinking
of St. Augustine

St. Augustine, (354-430 C.E.), was the Bishop of Hippo in North Africa. His views and copious writings probably made him second only to St. Paul in the formation of the doctrine and dogma of the Roman Catholic Church. In his infinite wisdom he wrote:

> "Nothing is to be accepted except on the authority of scripture, since greater is that authority than all powers of the human mind."

The presumptive intellectual error in Augustine's thinking is that Scripture, while written by priests and their functional analogs, had some kind of both Divine Guidance and Sanction, and therefore, was completely true and without fault or error. Nothing could be further from the truth. The details are for another time, but suffice it to say that, whole books written by competent Biblical scholars have shown that the countless contradictions, numerous inconsistencies, errors of fact, muddled chronologies, historical inaccuracies, evidence of interpolations and redactions make the claim of sanction and guidance by an omniscient deity to produce a Holy Text a preposterous assertion. An omniscient deity would never be responsible for such an internally incoherent, mishmash of unintelligible confusion.

But, what the hey! Priests have always made outrageous assertions to lend credibility and authority to their ideas meant to control the restless masses of ignorant, credulous people.

So much for arguments from authority.

Considering Augustine's statement we can legitimately ask:

Could any statement, from any source, possibly better illustrate the rigid, uncompromising, intolerant attitude of Christianity toward new knowledge?

Could any statement from an authority figure of Augustine's influence have done more damage to the spirit of human inquiry?

Could any statement have done more to slam the door on experimentation and research?

Could any statement have done more to retard the growth and development of Western Civilization?

Could any statement possibly have created a more hostile attitude toward rapprochement with other religions?

Could any statement have done more to denigrate and dehumanize human intelligence?

Could any statement have done more to initiate 1000 years of intellectual stagnation and regression that we have known as the Dark Ages?

One of the most revered and influential minds in the history of the Church has left a festering, intellectual open wound on Western Civilization.

We can do better. We must do better.

It was only when I finally undertook to read the Bible through from beginning to end that I perceived that its depiction of the Lord God—whom I had always viewed as the very embodiment of perfection—was actually that of a monstrous, vengeful tyrant, far exceeding in bloodthirstiness and insane savagery the depredations of Hitler, Stalin, Pol Pot, Attila the Hun, or any other mass murderer of ancient or modern history.

—"Steve Allen, Steve Allen on the Bible, Religion & Morality", 1990

~~~~~~~~~~~~~~~~~~~

The church says the earth is flat, but I know that it is round, for I have seen the shadow on the moon, and I have more faith in a shadow than in the church.

—As attributed to Ferdinand Magellan (1480-1521), Portuguese navigator, by Robert G. Ingersoll. Source: The Great Quotations edited by George Seldes.

~~~~~~~~~~~~~~~~~~~

In the long run nothing can withstand reason and experience, and the contradiction religion offers to both is only too palpable.

—Sigmund Freud (1856-1939), "The Future of an Illusion" (1927)

The Evolution of Gods, Violence, and Public Education

The natural progression of many gods to major and minor gods lead inevitably to a hierarchy of gods with a chief deity. From a chief deity to an only deity was then also inevitable. Monotheism was here to stay. The next step was, "My god is greater than your god."

The Egyptian Pharaoh Akhenaten (1379-1362 B.C.E.) superimposed his ideas of monotheism on all of his people who had been polytheistic for millennia. Akhenaten was never really successful convincing his people of his monotheistic ideas. When Akhenaten died, his supreme hegemony as Pharaoh died with him and the Egyptians reverted to their old polytheism. Statues of Akhenaten were vandalized and most remembrances of him were destroyed.

Other cultures produced monotheistic religions, most notably the Hebrews with their god, Yahweh or Jehovah. One god or many, this god or that, none of them had any more veracity than any of the others. Adopt the god of your parents, the god of the culture you grew up in, were indoctrinated with, or make up your own. It is, and has always been, a matter of "pick-'em-as-you-like-'em." Whatever god fits your purpose—whatever works for you. People have always created and defined their gods to suit them. In many millennia, nothing has changed in this regard.

In their endless and seemingly insatiable quest for power and dominion over others, adherents of monotheistic religions insist that all other gods but theirs are false gods. Labeled as heretics, or as blasphemers, all people who held alternative ideas were shunned, excommunicated, persecuted, demonized, castigated or killed. Thus, the roots of violence grow from the authoritarianism, the attendant intolerance, the bigotry and hatred of monotheistic absolutism.

Inevitably, it seems, contact between different monotheistic religions, or even variations within monotheistic religions produces a most virulent and invincible kind of intolerance. For confirmation of this thesis we need only to look at the Christian/Muslim conflict, The Catholic/Protestant situation in Ireland, The Hindu/Muslim conflict in India and Pakistan, The Sunni/Shiite hostility in the Muslim community, or the Roman Catholic vs. the Orthodox in Yugoslavia. Others abound aplenty—one kind of monotheistic crazy killing anything or anyone who holds a different view. Whenever absolutist religions based on the absolute truth of an Absolute Authority is confronted with any kind of alternative thinking or attitude, bloodshed soon follows.

The solution to the problem: We can either revert to the ignorance and superstition of polytheism, or we can adopt a modern scientific approach to understanding and explaining natural phenomena. We can ask ourselves how many people have been killed by using a religio/subjective means to assess reality. The answer is millions. Now ask, how many scientists have killed other scientists over a difference of opinion of their scientific/objective assessment of reality. The answer is none. At this point, has the message escaped anyone? We are faced with a choice of choosing between a religio/subjective approach to solving our problems that is committed to absolutism, and a scientific/objective approach that regards all truths to be tentative and provisional. Science easily accommodates an evolving culture, and adapts effortlessly to change and new knowledge. It is the nature of the scientific approach to do so, and there is no bloodshed. Religions are rigid, uncompromising, absolutist paradigms that flex and accommodate change and new knowledge only when forced by new realities, but too late to avoid the bloodshed inherent in absolutist world views.

The Catholic/Protestant hostility in Ireland, like the Jewish/Muslim hostility in Israel and other religious dichotomies around the world are irresolvable because both sides are wrong, and we all know that two wrongs never add up to a right. They are both wrong because they are both committed to absolutist philosophies derived from their absolutist religions that leave no latitude whatever for resolution.

Historically, people in their ignorance faced the mystery of the unknown in fear and dread. The causation of natural phenomena like lightning, tornadoes, earthquakes, and the wind were not understood at all. Objective explanations of these phenomena were not really possible from their frame of reference. Subjective, speculative explanations of misunderstood and misinterpreted natural phenomena became the roots of all religions. The sun, the moon, and other phenomena were explained in anthropomorphic terms and became the deities of polytheistic religions. There were gods and goddesses for this and for that—major deities and minor deities for every imaginable thing or idea. There were so many deities that when different cultures came into contact, the gods of both cultures had a great deal of overlap. Many gods were in common, but with different names. One or a few gods more or less than another culture was not a cause for concern, nor conflict. Absolutism cannot arise out of ambiguity, paradox or uncertainty.

Banishing monotheistic religions would seem to be a quick-fix solution, but that idea, like all simplistic solutions to complex issues, is not at all feasible. How to accomplish the goal of minimizing the destructiveness of absolutist paradigms for problem solving and adopting a scientific objective paradigm that eschews absolutes can be realized only by a commitment of society as a whole to a kind of quality scientific education of our children. This is obviously a long range goal. Since the major thrust of our culture is scientifically oriented, the goal of scientific literacy for all people becomes the educational imperative for everyone in the 21st century. Failing to answer this universal imperative in a productive way will guarantee the continuance of the failure of the religio/subjective paradigm for dealing with our most pressing problems.

In order for this plan to reach fruition the religious community must come to grips with the reality of our times. The time passed well over a hundred years ago when the religious community had any legitimate claim to primacy of authority about the physical and the factual. The religious explanations for natural phenomena have all been rendered invalid and inoperative by the inexorable advances of science. We must all accept the reality that any attempt to understand the true nature of natural phenomena can only be found in the scientific domain. The entire religious community must accept the reality that all authority about the physical and the factual of the cosmos is now in the scientific domain. All references to questions about the physical and the factual of the cosmos from Scripture have proven over and over to be catastrophically wrong. The time to correct this egregious intellectual error is now !

Unthinking respect for authority is the greatest enemy of truth.
—Albert Einstein

~~~~~~~~~~~~~~~~~~~

We have usurped many of the powers we once ascribed to God. Fearful and unprepared, we have assumed lordship over the life or death of the whole world—of all living things. The danger and the glory and the choice rest finally in man. The test of his perfectibility is at hand. Having taken Godlike power, we must seek in ourselves for the responsibility and the wisdom we once prayed some deity might have. Man himself has become our greatest hazard and our only hope. So that today, St. John the apostle may well be paraphrased: In the end is the Word, and the Word is Man—and the Word is with Men.
—John Steinbeck, Nobel Prize for Literature acceptance speech, 1962

~~~~~~~~~~~~~~~~~~~

Christianity persecuted, tortured, and burned. Like a hound it tracked the very scent of heresy. It kindled wars, and nursed furious hatreds and ambitions. It sanctified, quite like Mohammedanism, extermination and tyranny . . .
—George Santayana, philosopher (1863-1952), Little Essays, No. 107, Christian Morality.

The Evolution of Moral Values

Values do not spring out of a vacuum. Historically, values are relative and products of evolving human experience. Different values in different cultures are born of different environments and different circumstances. What is regarded as immoral or unethical in one culture isn't necessarily seen in the same context in another culture.

A constant state of flux in our culture and society requires constantly evolving values and criteria for what is moral and ethical. "Do's" and "don'ts" that were allegedly carved in stone several thousand years ago aren't necessarily the most appropriate for us today.

As humans, we reinterpret our circumstances to suit our needs and construct moral codes as needed. This is biologically and evolutionarily adaptive. While other organisms on this planet survive because they are adapted to their environment, humans adapt as needed to their environment.

Laws of any kind are intellectual constructs designed to produce societal stability which encourages the status quo. This doesn't always work because circumstances and environments change. We call this the evolution of moral standards.

New circumstances bring new moral codes. This will produce an erosion of strict obedience—the slippery slope. Moral agents of change are accused of "Playing God". Profound changes in moral standards demanded by some can lead to violence.

The world is changing whether we like it or not and whether we approve or not. We will be best served if we take a pro-active position and help direct the evolution of our moral and ethical standards. If we don't, others will do it for us, and we might not like what what they decide. We call this democratic governance.

To suggest that morals are from some external source, divine or otherwise, is insulting and denigrating to human intelligence and presumes that we as human beings are incapable of deciding, choosing and constructing our own moral code from collective community experience.

Oh, that the wise from their bright minds would kindle
Such lamps within the dome of this dim world
That the pale name of priest might shrink and dwindle
Into the Hell from which it first was furled.
 —Percy Bysshe Shelley (1792-1822), "Ode to Liberty," 1820

~~~~~~~~~~~~~~~~~~

The ethical view of the universe involves us at last in so many cruel and absurd contradictions . . . that I have come to suspect that the aim of creation cannot be ethical at all.
       —Joseph Conrad, (1912)

~~~~~~~~~~~~~~~~~~

"Religion is a mere castle in the air. Theology is ignorance of natural causes; a tissue of fallacies and contradictions." He believed: "Knowledge, Reason, and Liberty, can alone reform and make men happier." He optimistically predicted: "If the ignorance of nature gave birth to the gods, knowledge of nature is destined to destroy them."
  —Baron d'Holbach In Common Sense, by Thomas Paine.

~~~~~~~~~~~~~~~~~~

The belief that there is only one truth and that oneself is in possession of it seems to me the deepest root of all evil that is in the world.
      —German physicist Max Born.

The Quest for Certainty and Absolutes

The world is a chaotic place, and uncertainty can be quite scary. Earthquakes, thunderstorms, floods, hurricanes, tornadoes, lightning, tsunamis and disease are natural phenomena that were inexplicable to ancient humankind. They represented forces with a kind of power that was both awe inspiring and frightening. All too frequently they were lethal. Coping with the consequences of these natural phenomena was so problematical that they required special answers from the tribal authorities of early Man. These people were looked to as the source of wisdom and for solutions to the problems people had.

In order to maintain their position of hegemony in the tribe, authority figures (chiefs, kings, priests, shamans) provided answers for the ignorant masses. Providing answers was a part of their job. A priori answers, the product of the imaginations of the authority figures, were easy to make, and if necessary they could invoke one or more invisible, ineffable deities to lend credibility to their answers. This was the original revealed truth—authority figures decided what the answers would be, and it was declared the word of the tribal deity. To question or challenge the word of the deity was heresy—a sin punishable by death. The unbeatable power play combination of the tribal authorities, the king and the priests et. al., could control the ignorant but restless masses with a combination of fear, guilt, shame, sin and death.

The promise of a life everlasting in paradise following inevitable death, with the benevolent Father Figure for obedience, and the threat of eternal torment and pain for the disobedient or unrepentant was a powerful tool for controlling the imaginations and behavior of the illiterate masses. This indoctrination, when started in infancy makes images so indelible in the impressionable minds of children that by adolescence nearly every child is a captive of the world view they are given. Faith becomes the prime source of truth in their lives. Truth in their lives is derived subjectively and externally by others. Creative, objective, independent thought is stifled and discouraged. Skepticism of the claims of authority figures is taboo. Higher order thinking skills of analysis, synthesis and evaluation are preempted, and conformity to the prevailing doctrines and dogma are the norm. Aberrant thought or behavior results in severe punishment or banishment from one's society. The king and the priest have prevailed again. The certitude of faith provides the constancy, the predictability, and the stability so desperately desired in a world that is so unpredictable and chaotic.

Faith is a tool for survival, and consequently it was evolutionarily adaptive behavior. In the evolutionary process those features—structural, physiological or behavioral—that worked were those features that were selected for and conserved, albeit they may have been imperfect, and only marginally effective. Faith in a charismatic or powerful leader provides for social cohesion—a necessary behavior pattern if ignorant humans were to survive the challenges and vicissitudes of living and surviving in a chaotic world.

The certitude provided by faith, however, is a double-edged sword. Certitude in the hands of powerful people who are more interested in maintaining their position of authority and power than coping with innovative thought provides the grounds for absolutism. For authority figures to tolerate relativism, ambiguity, or paradox would invite instability, dissent, and innovative ideas. Consequently, everything is subject to change. Of course, this would severely compromise the power and control of the king and the priest. "The Word" is declared holy and sacred, immutable and transcendent. Growth and development is severely impacted in a negative way. Society stagnates. Cultures decline and are superseded by other cultures that are more flexible, more tolerant, more modern and less superstitious.

The certainty that provided so much comfort was also the origin of absolute truth. Absolute truth is the root of authoritarianism. Authoritarianism is intolerant of dissent, innovative thinking or the justice of democratic ideas which threaten the extant power regime. Authoritarianism begets totalitarianism which begets intolerance and bigotry. Bigotry is the source of persecution. Persecution in the extreme results in the violence that is the trigger for murder, war, and genocide.

The desire and the quest for certainty, while seemingly innocuous and innocent on the surface, can be the source of a cascade of unintended consequences that often result in disaster. It is in our collective interest to critically examine our appetite for absolutes and certainty. We need to understand that there are inherent risks in convenient comfort.

As we learned from our parents; be careful what you ask for—you may get it!

It is almost impossible to exaggerate the proneness of the human mind to take miracles as evidence, and to seek for miracles as evidence.
``` ` ` ` ` ` ` ```

The personages of the Christian heaven and their conversations are no more matter of fact than the personages of the Greek Olympus and their conversations.

—Matthew Arnold, "God and the Bible," preface, 1875.

~~~~~~~~~~~~~~~~~~~

"Nobody but a dedicated Christian could possibly read the gospels and not see them as a tissue of nonsense."

—Isaac Asimov. (Nov. 1, 1966 letter).

~~~~~~~~~~~~~~~~~~~

The sooner you get rid of all this Christian humbug the better. The whole traditional concept of life is false. Throw those great Christian blinkers away, and look around you and stand on your own feet . . . Don't believe all the tommyrot priests tell you; learn and prove everything by your own experience . . . One thing is certain—that English music will never be any good till they get rid of Jesus. Humanity is incredible. It will believe anything, anything to escape reality.

—Frederick Delius, "As I Knew Him," by Eric Fenby.
```

Archbishop Ussher, Religious Fundamentalism and Modern Science

There are hundreds and hundreds of creation myths from as many cultures around the world, and not one of them has any more veracity than any of the others. An interesting quirk about the Biblical account of creation, however, has left an indelible (if undeserved) impression on millions of people, especially the fundamentalists.

James Ussher, (1581-1656) the Archbishop of Armagh, Ireland, in his ecclesiastical zeal made an egregious error in his attempt to make his mark in history. The Bishop will always be remembered by Christians and non-Christians alike for making a monstrous intellectual blunder. He attempted to add credibility to the Biblical creation myth by adding objective quantification to a subjectively conceived myth. The resultant obfuscation still clouds our understanding of the story and the message.

Ussher, using all the "begats" in the genealogies of Genesis and the authority of his office, calculated in his own way that Adam was created in 4004 B.C.E. He also calculated that "The Flood" had occurred 1655 years later in 2349 B.C.E., but offered only a creation myth to support his views.

Accepting Ussher's views on faith as legitimate, John Lightfoot of Cambridge, in 1642, determined to leave his mark on history as well, declared that Adam had been created at precisely 9:00 a.m. on October 23, 4004 B.C.E. We are at a loss to know just how Lightfoot arrived at his audacious calculation.

Sometime between 1650 and 1654 Ussher published his Biblical chronology under the title "Annales Veteris et Novi Testamenti." In 1703 the dates he "calculated" were inserted into the margins of the

King James Version of the Bible. Since that time fundamentalists (and others) have eagerly grasped onto anything that would lend credibility to their literalist interpretation of their religious text. Today, no intelligent, educated person would accept Ussher's dates as legitimate, nor would they accept the idea that the world is less than 10,000 years old. Modern versions of the Bible have deleted the "data" by Ussher and Lightfoot.

Modern scientific knowledge about the physical and the factual make such ideas not only foolish, but absurd. In spite of modern, scholarly, critical evaluation of the Bible, a gross misinterpretation of the Bible still persists among fundamentalists—something like a pool of ignorance providing inspiration to the ignorant.

While we can justify looking to religion for guidance about things like ethics, morals, and life's choices, we must render unto science all primacy of authority about the physical and the factual—the objective and the quantifiable. To do otherwise is a cultural disaster with dire consequences.

Prayers are to men as dolls are to children. They are not without use and comfort, but it is not easy to take them very seriously.

—Samuel Butler.

~~~~~~~~~~~~~~~~~~

The most tedious of all discourses are on the subject of the Supreme Being.

—Ralph Waldo Emerson (1803-1882), journal, 1836.

~~~~~~~~~~~~~~~~~~

All life is problem solving . . . There are no absolutes; progress comes through critical thought . . . . Reason, not obedience, should guide our lives. Though it took centuries to crumble, the entire ossified cage of European social hierarchy—from kings to serfs, and between men and women, all of it shored up by the Catholic Church—was destroyed by this thought.

—Ayaan Hirsi Ali, "Infidel" (2007)

What is the Bible?

In my conversations over the years with friends and acquaintances on a wide range of philosophical subjects, both secular and religious, the topic of the Bible and its contents comes up with some frequency. There probably are few texts about which there is such a huge diversity of interpretation and opinion by both religious lay persons and professionals alike. It certainly would make matters a lot easier if we all understood it in the same context. However, there are those who are determined to read and try to understand the Bible from a simplistic and literal way in a defiant rejection of the highest levels of scholarship. Others take a more sophisticated and enlightened approach and get a substantially different perspective. Therein lies the rub.

What is the Bible? In spite of some of its positives, it is a collection of ancient, primordial visions and poetical figments of archaic imaginations. It reflects traditional tribal prejudices, subjective distortions, verbal confusions and intellectual obfuscations of an alien cultural Zeitgeist. It was written in near total ignorance of the physical and biological laws of the universe. It has been superseded by an expanded human knowledge base that has accrued in the past 2000 years.

The Bible is riddled with numerous inconsistencies, countless contradictions, and it defies a coherent understanding and interpretation of its message even by those who claim to know it best. It contains scores of metaphors, allegorical narratives, and symbolic references that were written in the context of the culture extant at that time. Most of these are poorly under-stood, if not completely misunderstood, by those who claim to have a firm grip

on a comprehensive understanding of the text. Others
different perspective and interpretation.

The Bible was written by people (men only) who were mc
concerned with providing "pictures for the mind" for the illiterate
masses than with the intellectual disputations so characteristic of
modern explication and scholarship.

The Bible contains scores of interpolations, redactions, errors
of fact, muddled chronologies and copyists errors. Historically, it
is a mishmash at best. Many of its meanings and lessons have been
lost, distorted, or misinterpreted in translation from languages that
have evolved contextually from the original editions.

The Bible is riddled with calculated ambiguities, literary tricks,
smudgy semantic stratagems, ecclesiastical politics and a healthy
dose of religious zealotry. All of this confusion is contained in a
tome that is supposed to inspire, lead, and advise.

There is even great disagreement over what books should be
included in the canon. The book of Luke was allegedly voted to
be included by just one vote. Whose or which Bible should we
accept as the sacred text? The Roman Catholic version? The King
James version? The Orthodox version? Others? Or none of the
above?

The Bible has been examined, scrutinized, analyzed, and
interpreted, ad infinitum, for centuries by professionals and lay
persons alike and still defies a clarified view of what is and what ought
to be, especially for our time and our cultural circumstances.

It has been alleged that it is the "Word of God," which is an
ancient and often used assertion made by priests to lend authority
to their ideas that they wanted to superimpose on the willful masses
even though no evidentiary support has ever been proffered to
support those assertions.

The Bible sanctions the beating of children, slavery, ownership
of concubines (sex slaves), and it regards women as property (like
livestock) and casts them as second class citizens. All of these,
and many more, are totally inconsistent with our contemporary
community standards.

The Bible demands the death penalty (by stoning or strangulation) for a long list of offenses such as working on the Sabbath or disrespecting one's parents even if they have been abusive. Messages of love and compassion are severely compromised and contradicted. Messages from a sacred text should be consistent and coherent. The Bible is neither.

Some people have suggested that we should adopt these ancient and archaic ideas advanced by those who wrote the Bible and were inspired by their god as appropriate mandates on how to live our lives in our culture and in our time. Given the above, it is easy to understand why this is so dangerous.

I think we can do better.

I have endeavored to dissipate these religious superstitions from the minds of women, and base their faith on science and reason, where I found for myself at least that peace and comfort I could never find in the Bible and the church . . . the less they believe, the better for their own happiness and development . . . .

For fifty years the women of this nation have tried to dam up this deadly stream that poisons all their lives, but thus far they have lacked the insight or courage to follow it back to its source and there strike the blow at the fountain of all tyranny, religious superstition, priestly power, and the canon law.

—Elizabeth Cady Stanton, "The Degraded Status of Woman in the Bible," 1896

The Christian religion not only was at first attended with miracles, but even at this day cannot be believed by any reasonable person without one.

—David Hume, "An Enquiry Concerning Human Understanding," 1748.

A man's ethical behavior should be based effectually on sympathy, education, and social ties; no religious basis is necessary. Man would indeed be in a poor way if he had to be restrained by fear of punishment and hope of reward after death.

—Albert Einstein.

Biblical Sexual Standards

Some Christian pastors have insisted that we should "return to Biblical standards" for governing our sexual propensities. Their position on this issue is predictable, lamentable and dangerous. On the surface this might seem to be a laudable idea, but after some reflective, critical thought, they leave us with some severely paradoxical problems.

"Biblical standards" (some Bronze Age, and some Iron Age) as a guide for constructing a modern code of sexual mores are hopelessly archaic, inconsistent with, and contradictory to a modern knowledge base and contemporary community standards. To employ such criteria would be to make an ethical/ moral mandate from a position of ignorance of all we have learned about ourselves and our world in the last several thousand years. We are reminded that a part of the definition of stupidity is the failure to incorporate newer information into our own knowledge base.

As illustrations, the Bible says that marriage shall consist of a union between one man and one, or more, women. (Genesis 29:17-28 and II Samuel 3:25). Marriage shall not impede a man's right to take concubines (sex slaves) in addition to his wife, or wives. II Samuel 5:13; I Kings 11:3; II Chronicles 11:21. Marriage shall be considered valid only if the wife is a virgin. If the wife is not a virgin, she is to be executed. Deuteronomy 22:13-21. The problem with employing Biblical standards for what ought to be is that the subscribers to such a code are literally forced to "cherry pick" their way through an intellectual morass of ancient and no longer appropriate standards trying to decide which are applicable to themselves and which are not. The critics bemoan the fact that there is much confusion about what is acceptable

170

sexual behavior, and what is not. It is not difficult to identify the source of the confusion. Moral codes for modern people must be derived from a modern knowledge base and consistent with contemporary community standards if we are to live in a rewarding and harmonious way.

While an argument can be made for sexual abstinence before marriage, (avoiding sexually transmitted diseases, e.g. syphilis, gonorrhea and AIDS) another argument can be made that says sex is for those who are prepared to live with the consequences. We are compelled to live with the cultural conundrum of teenagers who are sexually competent but who are not prepared to live with the consequences of sexual freedom. Freedom from any kind of restraints always demands a higher level of responsibility that can be understood and practiced only by appropriate education. Prescriptions and proscriptions about our ethical/moral behaviors without an adequate understanding of the "whys" and "wherefores" can never be expected to result in the desired behavioral modifications without relevant knowledge. Attempting to deal with the problem by "going back to Biblical standards" is not only cultural regression, it is socially dangerous.

Homosexuality is condemned in the Bible as an abomination. This behavioral proscription was made in ignorance of the scientific/ biological reality that homosexuality, while at variance with the norm, is a well documented natural phenomenon. Condemning people who are different through no fault of their own is bigotry. To suggest that homosexually oriented people are the way they are by choice, is not only an intellectual error, it is cruel and unjustifiably discriminatory. Declaring "Freedom and Justice for All" in America, and then condemning people for their biological variation is cognitive dissonance in the extreme. The confusion about homosexuality is the product of the ignorance on the subject derived from the Bible. Expecting to find guidance and understanding about natural phenomena from the Bible has a long (and bloody) history of abject failure. It is long past time when we need to come to grips with the fact that the Bible is a seriously flawed source of knowledge for governing our lives in our time.

We, with our modern scientific knowledge base, are better equipped and prepared to write and promulgate our own ethical/moral codes than those people from an ancient, archaic, superstitious, pre-scientific, tribal culture. We call it humanism.

One can assert with confidence that "God talk" and "Biblical standards" are hopelessly and tragically out of date. Consequently they are inappropriate for us in our culture, in our time.

Methinks sometimes I have no more wit than a Christian.
—William Shakespeare, "Twelfth Night,"
Act I, Sc. III

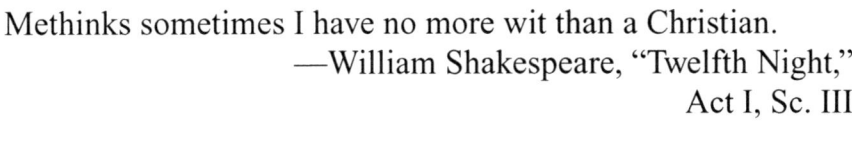

His worst fault is, he's given to prayer; he is something peevish that way.
—William Shakespeare—"The Merry Wives of Windsor,"
Act I, Sc. IV

To hate man and worship God seems to be the sum of all creeds.
—Robert G. Ingersoll, "Some Mistakes of Moses," 1879

The whole scheme of Christian salvation is diabolical as revealed by the creeds. An angry God, imagine such a creator of the universe. Angry at what he knew was coming and was himself responsible for. Then he sets himself about to beget a son, in order that the child should beg him to forgive the Sinner. This however he cannot or will not do. He must punish somebody—so the son offers himself up & our creator punishes the innocent youth, never heard of before—for the guilty and became reconciled to us . . . . I decline to accept Salvation from such a fiend.
—Andrew Carnegie, to Sir James Donaldson,
Principal of St. Andrews University, June 1, 1905.
Letters (except to Haldane) in Library of
Congress collection, cited by
Joseph Frazier Wall, Andrew Carnegie, 1970.

Dinosaurs, Christianity, Evolution and Extinction

Christianity has been the dominant religion in Western Civilization for nearly two thousand years. In the last hundred years or so, profound changes have occurred that dictate that adaptation to the changes will be necessary if Christianity is to avoid extinction. The factor that has dictated the necessity of change is called "modern science."

Science is now the prevailing paradigm for assessing, evaluating and explaining the natural phenomena of the world and the cosmos. The objective, the physical, and the factual in our lives cannot be adequately addressed or understood by the subjective, ancient, and archaic myths that reflect the ignorance, the tribal biases, and the superstitions of those who wrote the Bible. The Biblical "miracles" that defy and deny the known laws of the universe can no longer get credible recognition from educated people.

Our need to know "who" we are, and "why" we are, can remain in the realm of philosophy or religion along with the ethical and moral codes that help us govern how we should lead our lives. However, if we are to make intelligent, informed decisions about our place in the cosmos, "what" we are and "how" we came to be, can only be adequately answered by our understanding of natural phenomena, and we are a part of the world's natural phenomena. That objective understanding comes only from science.

Obsolescence is the reality of inevitable change in the history of the world. The history of the dinosaurs is the preeminent lesson for Christians. The dinosaurs were the dominant form of animal life on earth for one hundred fifty million years. When profound change occurred, they could not evolve and adapt fast enough to avoid extinction.

The message of the dinosaurs is clear and unequivocal: evolve and adapt to new scientific realities or face extinction.

. . . man has accomplished far more miracles than the God he invented. What a tragedy it is to invent a God and then suffer to keep him King.

—Rod Steiger, Playboy, July, 1969.

~~~~~~~~~~~~~~~~~~

This would be the best of all possible worlds if their were no religion in it.

—President John Adams

~~~~~~~~~~~~~~~~~~

My earlier views on the unsoundness of the Christian scheme of salvation have become clearer and stronger with advancing years, and I see no reason for thinking I shall ever change them.

—President Abraham Lincoln

The Jesus of the Gospels: History or Myth?

From our study of history and mythology we know that there were literally scores of pagan mystery religions that existed in the general area of the eastern Mediterranean Sea from Italy to the Indus River, and from Egypt to Russia.

These mystery religions existed in different versions for thousands of years before the Christian era. Nearly all of these mystery religions had in common a mythical, allegorical man-god hero figure who was known by different names in different areas and cultures. The original and oldest, as best we know, was Osiris from Egypt. From Egypt this mythology spread over the entire area. Among the Greeks the man-god was called Dionysus; in Persia, Mithra; in Asia Minor (Turkey), Attis; in Syria, Adonis; among the Romans, Bacchus; and others less well known.

While details varied from one of these mythical characters to another, there was a common motif shared by all of them according to Timothy Freke and Peter Gandy in their 1999 book, The Jesus Mysteries. The mythic motifs shared by all of these man-god hero figures are: They were God made flesh, the savior and "Son of God." His father is God and his mother is a mortal virgin. He is born in a cave or humble cow shed on Dec. 25th in the presence of three shepherds. He offers his followers a chance to be born again through the rights of baptism. He miraculously turns water into wine at a marriage ceremony. He rides triumphantly into town on a donkey while people wave palm fronds to honor him. He dies in springtime as a sacrifice for the sins of the world. After his death he descends to hell, then on the third day he rises from the dead and ascends to heaven in glory. His followers await his return as the judge during the Last Days. His death and resurrection are celebrated by a ritual meal of bread and wine, which symbolize his body and blood.

This all sounds so familiar. If we plug the Jesus of Nazareth story from the Gospels into the common motif of the pagan mythological mystery religions, we suddenly convert a mythical, allegorical hero figure into a historical, literal hero figure.

The inconceivable has just become conceivable. It appears that the Jesus of Nazareth story of the Gospels is an ancient pagan myth that has been appropriated, reconstructed and repackaged to advance a newer religious agenda.

If only there were some reliable and confirmable evidence from some source other than the gospels to support the assertion that the Jesus of the gospels was a historical person, Christianity could be standing on a firm footing. Alas, there is none.

It is arguable that there was a historical Jesus, but according to some of the best informed recent scholarship, the Jesus of the gospels is essentially mythological fiction.

Linguistic, literary and computer analysis of the writings of Flavius Josephus, (aka Yousef ben Matityahu [Yousef son of Matthias]) have shown that the brief reference to a Jesus figure were interpolations that were added by Christians several hundred years later to give credence to their religious myth.

There is no evidence in Roman records to support the gospel story that the hated Pontius Pilate, the brutal Roman Prefect of Judea at the alleged time of Jesus' death, had anything to do with any trial or execution of a Jesus figure.

Bishop Eusebius, the propagandist of the early church, unabashedly admitted that his altogether fictional accounts of persons, places and accounts of events to further his religious agenda were means that justified his desired ends. Academic honesty and intellectual integrity were not a high priority of those advancing an ideological cause.

Saul of Tarsus, aka St. Paul, was a Hellenized Jew, who knew of the pagan hero figures of the mystery religions, but never met any man named Jesus of Nazareth.

The Jesus of the gospels never wrote anything, and never put his name to any writing. We have no accurate idea when he was born, and no reliable date for his death or any other event in his life.

The alleged Apostles were all illiterate, and no one knows who wrote the gospels. None of the authors had ever seen or known a Jesus character. The earliest gospel, Mark, was allegedly written about year 70 C.E. and the others a generation or two later. Deletions, interpolations and redactions of the gospels before the canon was finalized created serious problems of authenticity and credibility.

Freke and Gandy provide a list of 27 names of pagan writers who wrote at, or within a century of the time that Jesus is said to have lived, but not one of them refers to a Jesus in spite of his many "miracles" that would have made a public scene.

Of the hundreds of "gospels" that were written, only the three Synoptic gospels and the Book of John were included in the final canon of the New Testament that was finalized by St. Athanasius in the year 367 C.E. In all likelihood the others were too problematical. Within the gospels themselves there are numerous profound inconsistencies and contradictions in the stories about Jesus of Nazareth.

Albert Schweitzer, the great physician, philosopher, Humanitarian and Nobel Peace Prize winner, wrote:

"There is nothing more negative than the result of the critical study of the life of Jesus. The Jesus of Nazareth who came forward publicly as the Messiah, who preached the ethic of the kingdom of God, who founded the kingdom of heaven on earth, and died to give his work its final consecration, never had any existence. This image has not been destroyed from without, it has fallen to pieces, cleft and disintegrated by the concrete historical problems which came to the surface one after the other."

It would seem that the case for a historical Jesus of the gospels gets weaker and weaker as newer, critical scholarship reveals the truth. Among the cognoscenti, the case for a historical Jesus of the gospels has collapsed, and it is crumbling for the rest.

Our myths and symbols, our metaphors and allegories, will always be an important part of human culture; however, we must recognize them for what they are and teach them as such. To do otherwise is a disservice to our children. There is a profound difference between education and indoctrination.

Among the millions of species that have evolved on earth over the past three and a half billion years, we are the only species that could be known as "Truth Seekers." It is time we lived up to our title.

"Here the ways of men part: if you wish to strive for peace of soul and pleasure, then believe; if you wish to be a devotee of truth, then inquire."

—Friedrich Wilhelm Nietzsche

~~~~~~~~~~~~~~~~~

When I started understanding how science works, it occurred to me that there just is no evidence that there is a God.

—Ben Bova, Interview on Freethought Radio, July 18, 2009

~~~~~~~~~~~~~~~~~

Examine the religious principles which have, in fact, prevailed in the world, and you will scarcely be persuaded that they are anything but sick men's dreams.

—David Hume 1748

Rethinking the God Hypothesis
in the 21st Century

Since all atoms and molecules are constantly in motion and frequently interacting spontaneously, the omnipresent characteristic of the cosmos is that it is constantly in a state of flux. Since this is observably so, the earth is constantly changing. The phenomenon of plate tectonics and the fossil record speak loudly and clearly to this reality. The question that confronts us now is, "How will we understand, explain and accommodate this perpetual state of dynamic change?"

Inasmuch as invoking any of 20,000 or so deities from religious mythology has been a demonstrated failure in explaining natural phenomena, modern, educated people have been employing the palpable success of the scientific paradigm to understand and explain those phenomena.

While present data indicate that modern Homo sapiens sapiens has been a part of the world's biota for about 50,000 years, our civilized, cultural history is little more than ten thousand years old since the advent of agriculture. For the vast majority of our history human beings survived as hunter-gatherers and/or pastoralists. Then the invention of agriculture changed everything in a very profound way. This was the necessary cultural step toward civilization—living in permanent villages or cities.

Although people seem predisposed to loving stasis for the constancy, certainty and predictability they seem to crave, the record of the changes in our history is replete with both minor paradigm shifts and revolutionary cultural quantum leaps. While the human mind is capable of making substantial adjustments to new realities, change of any kind can result in angst and fear, largely of the unknown and unpredictable future.

While some people seem to adjust to changing vicissitudes better than others, most people seek reassurance from a parent figure, real or imagined, who will ameliorate their fears borne of the ignorance, uncertainty and ambiguity of their lives. Consequently, they can be easily exploited by the more assertive, even aggressive, members of their society who assume, or take by force, the mantle of the parent figure, the "Protector/Provider."

There are two kinds of people who separate themselves from the masses to occupy this cultural niche. The first is the "king," or "chief," or "pharaoh," or "emperor." They occupy a singular position that is often deified and advertised as all powerful, even infallible. These are the "alpha" people—nearly always men. They are the supreme authority in all matters. They have an insatiable appetite for power and control over all others. Their word is law and dissent is summarily crushed. The second type of person who seeks dominion over others is the priest/bishop. These are the "beta" people. These are the control freaks who use guile, propaganda, deception, deceit and mendacity to exercise their nefarious agenda. Priests organize themselves into hierarchies and vie for control with the king and his court. The association is tenuous and shifting, depending on the strength of the power hungry personalities. The king and the priest have always found it to their advantage to live in a symbiotic relationship with the other. The king had the sword, (objectivity) and the priests had their tools of fear, guilt, shame, sin and the threat of death (subjectivity) as they exploited the ignorance, naiveté and superstition of the masses. Together they had an unbeatable power combination to control the sometimes volatile and unruly masses.

Today we use the names "President" and "Pope" as euphemisms for the king and the priest, but the outcome is still largely unchanged as the alpha people and the beta people sort out who will have what kind of authority to manipulate the masses to their purpose. The alpha people and the beta people conspire to dole out just enough of the communal pie to the masses to keep them pacified and just short of open revolt. In all of human history the stronger have always exploited the weaker to their purpose. To emphasize to the masses their role as "protector", it is often necessary to invent/create a crisis by frightening the masses with an evil menace. Then they whip up the masses with propaganda about the threat with appeals to unbridled patriotism and flaming religious zeal. This has been the formula for the ruling class for centuries and is still the tactic of choice for tyrants.

Human beings evolved as social primates from non-human primates because they could not have survived as solitary animals. The glue that held this often tenuous association together was a predilection to be believers—to be followers. Without this predilection to believing and following, it is highly unlikely that early hominids could have survived the hazards of the world's natural environment as solitary animals.

The leaders, the alpha and the beta people decided what everyone was to believe, how to act, and the masses obeyed and followed. It was in their collective interests to do so if they were to survive. However, human beings, mostly the males, are what they are and their androgens sometimes got out of hand. Many were prone to abuse their position of absolute power. As Lord Acton said, "Power corrupts and absolute power corrupts absolutely." The more intellectually astute members of the masses sought a bigger piece of the pie and more say in their governance. These people were labeled as unpatriotic and heretical. More often than not, these rebellions were crushed with force. Ignorance and superstition were the greatest liabilities of the masses. Keeping the masses ignorant, superstitious, and frightened were the prime requisites for controlling them. This is called maintaining the status quo. The perpetuators and promulgators of ignorance, superstition, and magical thinking have always been an absolute monarch and as many priests as the king could control.

To solidify their control, the priests organized and sanctified their agenda and called it "religion." They asserted (without any evidence) to the masses that the Holy Book they had written was inspired by the deity they had created. The priests said this was what the masses were to believe, and the believers said, in the interests of social cohesion, "We believe!" The natural xenophobic tendency of humans was exacerbated. Human beings saw themselves as "us" vs. "them." Religion had become a divisive agent of our culture. Since the priests desired absolute control, they claimed to have absolute truth. All other views or interpretations were labeled as evil, heretical and/or blasphemous. Those who would not recant their opposing views were slaughtered in order to purge society of evil influences.

The priests at all levels in their hierarchy have had centuries to polish their crafts and methodologies. Defenses were solidified and apologists trained. They became so skilled and polished in their craft that few if any could sustain a concerted or protracted attack. The priests became so entrenched that they became almost invulnerable. But change was inevitable and cracks began to appear in the priestly armor. The mortal enemies of the priests and their religion were reason, logic, and critical thinking. Dogma was seen as authoritarian instead of authoritative. Rigid doctrines proved to be vulnerable in the light of critical examination. As the collective knowledge base increased, self-determination became a more common idea among those with the most mental acuity. Intellectual ferment became the rule, not the exception. Cultural evolution accelerated. New ideas that surfaced represented new threats to the status quo. Reform and revolution resulted in profound changes at all levels of society.

While the priests lost a great deal of power with the more liberal-minded people, they found refuge and solace among those with a propensity for a conservative view of reality. Thus, these promulgators and perpetuators of ignorance, superstition, and spiritual poverty are still with us today. Con artists will always, it seems, find and exploit the credulous and the gullible with their fantastical tales that deny and defy the known laws of the natural universe. Since gods, religions, theologies, and their ghastly derivatives are the product of irrational priestly thought, we cannot expect that anything better will come from their arrested cognitive development and subsequent cultural retardation. The great French encyclopedist and philosopher Denis Diderot said it best when he wrote, "Man will never be free until the last king is strangled with the guts of the last priest."

Since religions are ancient, archaic thinking derived from an alien culture in total ignorance of all we have learned in the last several millennia, we have to ask, "Why have religions been so successful even to this day in view of the fact that they are so obviously illogical and irrational?" The answer seems to be that people will believe almost anything proffered to them by an authority figure who will promise comfort and assuage their fears if they will only believe their ludicrous fictions as historical and factual. Truly, theology and its attendant rituals are candy for the limbic system of the believers.

For all of human history until the last several hundred years, the kings and the priests have superimposed their uncritical intellectual and emotional tyranny on the credulous masses. Now, with the advantages of the histories of the Renaissance, the Reformation and the Enlightenment in our rearview mirror, and with the Sci/Tech Revolution still making almost incomprehensible quantum leaps forward, we are compelled to make an even more critical examination of what we believe about the world and the cosmos as defined by the still prevailing philosophical paradigm of our culture—religion.

Given the phenomenon of consciousness as a part of human intelligence and the immanent human propensity as truth seekers, we find a need for a dependable model or paradigm to evaluate incoming information and weigh it against our experience. Those in control have historically been those who decided what the truth-seeking model or paradigm would be. Since the invention of writing (probably in the Sumerian culture of the lower Tigris-Euphrates river valleys ca. 3500 BCE) the only literate people were the king and the priests. The priests (always being preoccupied with advancing their religious ideology) were hardly given to objective analysis and evaluation of the physical and the factual of the natural phenomena of their daily lives. On the contrary, in the complete absence of any kind of scientific paradigm, the priests, with their subjective approach to problem solving, explained natural phenomena by invoking various gods, demons, devils, poltergeists or other supernatural agents. As truth seekers who needed an explanation for everything, even if the track record of the priests was wanting, the status quo prevailed for the masses. Change of any kind only added to the uncertainty and ambiguity of their lives. Hence, the conservative position so characteristic of priestly thinking was, and is, a major factor that chronically retarded cultural advance. We are still paying a heavy price for allowing priestly influence to keep its foot on the brake of the scientific engines of cultural advance.

The Renaissance was a reawakening of the human creative spirit that finally ended a thousand years of intellectual stagnation that was spawned from the priestly thinking of the Roman Catholic Church. At this point in our history we can only speculate as to how far Western Civilization might have progressed after the intellectual spark from the Greeks made such a glorious cultural leap beyond barbarism, only to be snuffed out by the absolutist ideology of the Roman Catholic religion in the hands of the Roman Emperor Constantine. If Constantine had not adopted Christianity as the official religion of the Roman Empire and sanctioned the authority of the Pope, Christianity may very well have suffered the same well-deserved death of the other mystery religions so common around the Mediterranean Sea in the first five hundred years of our Common Era.

Never was the Law of Unintended Consequences so well exemplified by the historically egregious error of allowing the Pope to get in bed with the Emperor. This catastrophic error made whores of both of them. All of us accept the fact that we will have to pay a price for our own mistakes, but while we are still paying for the errors of judgment of Roman Emperor Constantine, we will be allowed to speculate on how long we will pay for the errors in judgment of President George W. Bush and his unindicted coconspirator in war crimes, Dick Cheney. Unconstrained power in the hands of an ambitious ideologue has always been a blueprint for disaster.

The rate of change seems to accelerate with every scientific and technological leap forward. Communication has made such advances that the dissemination of knowledge, both old and new, has become available to nearly everyone, even in remote places.

Ideas that for so long took months or years to go from one part of the globe to another are now disseminated worldwide in fractions of seconds. More than ever before, we are compelled to reexamine what we thought was true. Wholesale changes in cultural norms are inducing angst, even fear. For many people this culture shock is so traumatic that they seem overwhelmed by it all. Keeping up with the flow is difficult for them. Comfort and succor become high priorities. Historically, that comfort came from the religious myths that were a part of all cultures. While these religious myths satisfied a perceived need for much of human history, they are no longer a valid part of our knowledge base. Old ideas are frequently rendered null and void in the light of new knowledge. We can no longer find legitimate, meaningful solace in ancient, archaic myths. We must compose modern, intellectually justified stories that address our emotional needs as we abandon outdated tales conceived in total ignorance of all we have learned about ourselves, the world, and the cosmos in the last millennium. Expecting to find meaningful answers to our needs in an ancient tome derived from an alien zeitgeist is blatant foolishness.

There is much in the Bible against which every instinct of my being rebels, so much so that I regret the necessity which has compelled me to read through from beginning to end. I do not think that the knowledge I have gained of its history and sources compensates me for the unpleasant details it has forced upon my attention.

—Helen Keller

~~~~~~~~~~~~~~~~~~

To discover the true principles of morality, men have no need of theology, of revelation, or of gods. They need but common sense. They have only to look within themselves, to reflect upon their own nature, to consult their obvious interests, to consider the object of society and of each of the members who compose it, and they will easily understand that virtue is an advantage, and that vice is an injury to beings of the species.

—Paul Henri Thiery, Baron d'Holbach 1723-1787.

Is The Bible the Word of an Omniscient God?

Probably the most intellectually indefensible assertion in human history is the commonly held idea that the Judeo-Christian Bible is the word of an omniscient deity, most commonly referred to as "God." This cannot possibly be true to even those with modest intellects. Still, this idea, indelibly impressed on credulous, young minds (and gullible old ones) for a lifetime is difficult for most people to abandon. Religious indoctrination can leave deep psychological scars. It is child abuse in any other guise.

A sacred text, written or inspired by an omniscient deity as a guide for living, would be: clear and unambiguous, devoid of inconsistencies and contradictions, historically and geographically accurate, temporally precise and accurate, identified clearly by author and be written reflecting a high level of modern scholarship that would not reflect ancient tribal jealousies and biases. None of these criteria have been met in the Bible. Consequently, to even suggest that the Bible was authored, or even inspired by, an omniscient deity is utterly defenseless. Preaching to the ignorant, credulous masses and indoctrinating them with this falsehood is a crime against humanity. This is a moral issue.

Truth is simple, error is complicated, uncertain in its gait, full of byways. The voice of nature is intelligible, that of falsehood is ambiguous, enigmatical, and mysterious.
—Paul Henri Thiery, Baron d'Holbach 1723-1787.

~~~~~~~~~~~~~~~~~

The road of truth is straight, that of imposture is oblique and dark. This truth, always necessary to man, is felt by all just minds. The lessons of reason are followed by all honest souls.
—Paul Henri Thiery, Baron d'Holbach 1723-1787.

~~~~~~~~~~~~~~~~~

In those parts of the world where learning and science have prevailed, miracles have ceased; but in those parts of it that are barbarous and ignorant, miracles are still in vogue.
—Ethan Allen

Jesus of Nazareth: True or False?

May we think about the unthinkable? Jesus was/is not a historical person, and yes, Jesus is a mythological man/god hero figure from the Middle East very much like dozens of others of that era of ignorance. A critical, scholarly consideration of all of the evidence for and against the case for a historical Jesus leads inevitably to the conclusion that has been known for over a hundred years: there was no historical Jesus. The icon of human perfection, created by and polished by Christian zealots with an agenda of mind control of the masses has been a success story of almost unimaginable magnitude. A masterpiece of fiction sold as factual history to credulous masses for centuries has run its course and no longer is regarded by educated people as anything more than an ancient religious myth. For all of its alleged holy virtues, the Jesus story in the gospels is fraudulent.

While our assessment is made outside of absolute certainty, no one knows whether there was or was not a man named Jesus in what we now know as Israel in the first century C.E. However, our only real source of information about this character named Jesus is from the Gospels, and inarguably, the Gospels are religious mythology. There is no reliable external corroboration that might validate this religious narrative.

The Biblical authors were not even trying to create an accurate history as we understand academic historians. Their objective was to create a story that was more like pictures for the mind for the illiterate masses. They had a religious/ideological agenda to advance in the first century, not a historical record for twenty first century critics.

Eusebius, a Roman Catholic bishop and church historian during Constantine's reign as Roman Emperor admitted in writing that he had no problem telling lies as long as those lies would advance their religious agenda. This is damning evidence against Biblical veracity.

The gospel attributed to Mark was written, according to Biblical scholars, about the year 70 C.E. The author of the gospel of Matthew (who borrowed extensively from Mark) was written about 90 C.E., and Luke was written about 100 C.E., probably by the author of Acts. The Gospel of John was written in a sharply contrasting style by a much more literate author probably later than 120 C.E. Since none of the disciples (albeit mythical) would have been literate, we have no certain knowledge about who the real authors of the gospels were, nor exactly when they were written. The dates for the writing of the gospels were estimated by literary analysis by Biblical scholars.

The entire Jesus story is shrouded in the dense fog of religious myth. None of it has any more historical veracity than other myths of that time frame. However, people will believe virtually anything, no matter how absurd or irrational, if they learned it from a recognized authority figure, (parents, priests and pastors) and especially if the story is consistent with their preconceived ideas. If a story is what they want to believe (for their own reasons) they will believe it. If it makes them feel good, or if it assuages their fears—all the better. The priesthood has had centuries to polish their craft. Manipulating uncritical, unsophisticated minds is easy for highly trained priests. It is easy to lead sheep to slaughter.

The Jesus story is a fictional allegory cobbled together from many antecedent pagan myths that was designed to create an idealistic icon who will promise miserable, desperate people that they can survive the death of their body and spend eternity in a state of perpetual bliss with a patriarchal father figure and their long-dead loved ones. Of course, this is all conditional on strict obedience to the mandates of the fictional man/god hero figure named Jesus who stood taller than any earthly priest.

The model for a savior is the product of creative "priest-speak." While the king might use brute force and the threat of death to enforce his rule, the priests controlled people's behavior by messing with their minds. Their tools were fear, guilt, shame, and sin. It is a remarkably effective strategy for manipulating credulous people. It has worked well for centuries on naive, uncritical minds. The skeptics, however, saw all of this for what it really was—fiction, fraud, and forgery. But people love their icons, illusions, and dreams even if they have no test in reality. For the believers, it probably doesn't even really matter if Jesus was a historical reality or the product of priestly imagination—they love their religious icon. Most people are more comfortable with their soft, warm, fuzzy, fictional illusions than the uncomfortable realities of their life. For most people, denial and self delusion are the favored means of dealing with life's hard realities and unpleasantness.

In the light of modern Biblical scholarship by dedicated believers, the reality of Jesus as a fictional, mythical character is being accepted by more and more people who identify themselves as truth-tellers. How much and what kind of impact this new reality will have on Christian thinking remains to be seen.

Our senses and our intellect—our reason—reveal nothing of any god. If we know nothing about any god through our intellect and senses the only thing we know about religion is what others have told us we are to believe. When others tell us what we are supposed to believe it is invariably in their interests, not ours. This should raise a red flag.

L. Rodney Sheffer

~~~~~~~~~~~~~~~~~~~~

We can get a clearer view of the truth of a proposition if we can compare the probability of scientific findings based on compelling evidence that has been repeatedly verified on the same epistemological continuum to the religious miracles that deny and defy the known laws of the universe.

L. Rodney Sheffer

~~~~~~~~~~~~~~~~~~~~

Since beliefs (usually acquired at an early age) determine one's perception of reality, absurd or irrational religious beliefs are very likely to result in seriously flawed judgements that affect policy decisions. Congress comes to mind.

L. Rodney Sheffer

~~~~~~~~~~~~~~~~~~~~

Religious faith is submitting to believing in impossible events and concepts that are repugnant to modern scientific thought, and a rejection of new knowledge.

L. Rodney Sheffer

Are Gods and Religion in Our Future?

The phenomenon of human intelligence and its attendant feature called consciousness demands that there be an explanation for everything. That the explanation does not necessarily pass the test of reality in most people's minds is not the most important thing—what matters is that there is an explanation.

All gods are the product of human imagination and exist only in the minds of the believers. Gods were created by people—usually priests or kings—to satisfy a perceived need or desire. Products of an unscientific age of ignorance, gods of any kind are pure mythology and fail all tests in reality. Probably one of the most egregious intellectual errors in human history is the transmogrification of mythology into historical fact. When people keep repeating the same kinds of errors and expecting different outcomes, we call this stupidity. Gods of any kind, from any culture, at any time, are Neolithic thinking. This cannot serve the best interests of either individuals or society as a whole in our time. Voltaire said it best: "Those who can make you believe in absurdities can make you commit atrocities." The indoctrination of children with irrational, illogical ideas about "gods" corrupts their cognitive processes and leads them into a lifetime of intellectual error. Only a small minority of people are ever able to shed this mantle of ignorance and emotional dependency. We continue to corrupt the minds of our children with intellectual garbage and then wonder why they have so much difficulty thinking in a way that would make them first-class problem solvers.

When these intellectually handicapped people become adults, some seek positions of power. Consequently, our legislatures are stocked with people whose minds are corrupted by the irrationalities and absurdities so common in religious convictions. Expecting that conclusions and decisions from such people can serve our best interests is seriously flawed because the process is shrouded in the obfuscations of myth and superstition. Critical/rational thought has been compromised by religious ideologies, miracles, and magical thinking. We can never expect to have laws, statutes, ordinances, regulations or policies that are in our collective best interests as long as religion is the common prevailing paradigm in our society.

The next necessary step in our cultural evolution is secularization if we are to survive the destructive and baleful effects of religious thought. The question before us now is, "Will we make the necessary change to secular thought as the dominant and prevailing intellectual paradigm in our society before we self-destruct under the pernicious effects of religious thinking?"

The conservative political correctness of Creationists may always exist in the realm of ancient abstractions, but in their lifesaving laboratories, scientists will always operate on the basis of Darwinian methodological empiricism, not Bible-based, theological speculations.

—Author Unknown

~~~~~~~~~~~~~~~~~~~~~

The biggest advantage to believing in God is you don't have to understand anything, no physics, no biology. I wanted to understand.

Every time you understand something, religion becomes less likely. Only with the discovery of the double helix and the ensuing genetic revolution have we had grounds for thinking that the powers held traditionally to be the exclusive property of the gods might one day be ours . . . .

—Nobel Laureate James Watson,
Youngstown State University speech,
quoted in The Vindicator, Dec. 2, 2003.

Is the Bible Historically Accurate?

Those Christian believers who imagine that the Gospels were written as eyewitness accounts have been misled and misinformed by ignorant and unqualified people. Even a cursory examination of the highest level of scholarship about the gospels makes abundantly clear that the gospel Mark was written not earlier than the year 70 C.E., Matthew and Luke sometime between the years 90-120 C.E., and John some decades later. No one knows who wrote the gospels. None of the authors have ever been identified by the highest levels of scholarship.

The contradictions and inconsistencies in the gospels about the alleged man/god hero figure named Jesus negate entirely the claim that the gospel stories were eyewitness narratives and historically accurate.

The scores of interpolations, redactions, errors of fact, muddled chronologies and copyist errors make claims of historical veracity of the gospels an intellectually indefensible assertion that should have disappeared along with the Christian myth centuries ago.

Internally incoherent and consequently open to unconstrained interpretation, conceived by myth makers and devoid of verifiable information, the gospels are not and have never been reliable history.

The gospels (and the Bible as a whole) were not written by what we would call academic historians who were trying dispassionately, as best they could, to create an accurate record of the past. The Bible was written by religious ideologues, who were dedicated to advancing a religious agenda—not factual history. Their mystical, mythological, allegorical narratives based on subjective speculation and unsubstantiated conjecture were and are as far from factual history as any other mythology. Expecting the gospels to be factually and historically accurate is an exercise in intellectual futility.

The refutation of the gospels (and the Bible as a whole) as historically factual, did not come from atheists—it came from theologians who were committed to finding the real truth. It was long overdue.

Believe nothing just because a so-called wise person said it. Believe nothing just because a belief is generally held. Believe nothing just because it is said in ancient books. Believe nothing just because it is said to be of divine origin. Believe nothing just because someone else believes it. Believe only what you yourself test and judge to be true.

—Buddha—Hindu Prince Gautama Siddhartha

~~~~~~~~~~~~~~~

I cannot see how a man of any large degree of humorous perception can ever be religious—except he purposely shut the eyes of his mind and keep them shut by force.

—Mark Twain, *Notebooks and Journals.*

~~~~~~~~~~~~~~~

I see no light behind that terrible curtain. I do not think one religion better than another, and I think the Christian religion has brought far more misery, crime, and suffering, far more tyranny and evil, than any other.

—Eliza Lynn Linton, letter to clergyman, 1897

~~~~~~~~~~~~~~~

I cannot believe in the immortality of the soul . . . . I am an aggregate of cells, as, for instance, New York City is an aggregate of individuals. Will New York City go to heaven . . . . No; nature made us—nature did it all—not the gods of the religions.

—Thomas Alva Edison, The New York Times, Oct. 2, 1910

Scientific or Religious Epistemologies?

In any venue of honest and rigorous intellectual disputation, whether academic, scientific, commerce, business, jurisprudence or any other, the closest approximation of truth hinges entirely on compelling evidence, verification and external corroboration. Our modern culture is absolutely predicated on these governing principles. When these objective criteria are not met, educated people regard claims of truth as being cognitively worthless and devoid of merit.

Attempts to arrive at the truth of a matter without the satisfaction of these criteria opens the door to all kinds of mischief, mayhem and bloodshed because purely subjective assessments of reality allow for an unlimited range of interpretations, and thus consensus is impossible. Absurdities, incongruities, anachronisms, irrationalities, and logically bizarre notions can and do hold sway. Consequently agreements about what is true, right, or good become impossible.

Religious doctrines and dogmas (beliefs), however, make no attempt whatever to satisfy these intellectual standards of truth telling. Instead, we witness ancient, archaic metaphors and misunderstood symbols, combined willy-nilly with mystical, mythological, allegorical narratives derived from the fears, ignorance, superstitions and magical thinking of an alien zeitgeist proffered millennia ago by ideological zealots with a religio/political agenda as factual history. Then an attempt is made to dignify this incomprehensible and indecipherable conglomeration of pottage by calling it "theology."

Without the rigorous intellectual discipline of the scientific paradigm, which is the most reliable and dependable means of truth determination ever conceived, we are adrift in a sea of subjective variables, unverifiable claims, unsupported assertions and intellectual quagmires with no prospect of ever arriving at reliable truths about the physical and the factual of the earth and the cosmos.

Certainly there is an element of subjective/intuitive thinking and leaps of imagination in the creative aspect of scientific enterprise. However, we must keep in mind that before the discoveries of science become a part of our common knowledge base, the findings of science are rigorously examined and scrutinized by skeptics, and repeated, objective verification and confirmation are required before we accept the findings as tentative and provisional scientific truth. Can we say the same for the assertions of revealed religion.

The harm that I see in religions in general, and the monotheistic religions in particular, is their need to have absolute truths that are not to be challenged or even questioned. This effectively shields the believers from any new knowledge or contrary evidence that might challenge their faith. The power of the hierarchy must be maintained at all costs. The result is intellectual tyranny and cultural regression. Also to be considered is that this kind of authoritarianism corrupts the cognitive processing of children. This results in a stunted mind trapped in a kind of intellectual channel that has neither depth nor breadth and fails to recognize the necessity of making conclusions on the evidence instead of on archaic dogmas. The open horizon of a child's imagination is suffocated by the darkness of a closed mind. Children don't deserve to be treated that way, and society cannot afford this intellectual error.

The most savage controversies are those about matters as to which there is no good evidence either way. Persecution is used in theology, not in arithmetic.

—Bertrand Russell (1872-1970), British author, philosopher, "An Outline in Intellectual Rubbish," Unpopular Essays (1950)

~~~~~~~~~~~~~~~~~~

All thinking men are atheists.

—Ernest Hemingway

~~~~~~~~~~~~~~~~~~

Arrogance comes in a variety of forms. The arrogance of great wealth; the arrogance of great power, and the arrogance of a great master are bearable because they rest on an acknowledged base. The arrogance of ignorance, however, is unbearable because it is rooted in smug satisfaction of being isolated from the facts of the case. The antievolution plank in the platform of Christian fundamentalism is a classic case of the arrogance of know-nothings.

—Biologist William V. Mayer 1984

A Letter to 21st Century Parents

If you want your children to be as ignorant about the world and the cosmos as you are—send them to the same Sunday School indoctrination center that corrupted your mind with all of the irrationalities, superstitions and magical thinking of your monotheistic religion.

Instead of teaching your children to approach the claims and assertions of alleged authority figures with a healthy degree of skepticism, indoctrinate them to believe and obey those who would channel their thinking into the same intellectual rut you are in.

Instead of teaching them to be independent thinkers and competent problem solvers, indoctrinate them with ideas from your religion that will produce robotic, knee-jerk reactions to the circumstances in their lives instead of reflective, analytical thinking.

Instead of teaching children that they are deserving of all of the love and the best that our modern culture can provide, indoctrinate them with the emotional and intellectual cancer that they are rotten, unworthy sinners in the eyes of an imaginary all powerful deity in the sky who will punish them everlastingly in a fiery Hell for their childish errors. Then you can wonder in ignorance why your children have such low self esteem.

Instead of educating your children with the idea that they are intelligent, competent and capable of achieving their dreams, tell them daily that they are dumb because their performance was less than perfect the first time they tried to do something the way you wanted it done. Then you can commiserate with others like yourself because your kids are not blue chip people.

Instead of insisting that they not only become scientifically literate, but scientifically competent, to live and function effectively in our scientific culture, indoctrinate them with the ideas from an ancient and archaic text that will assure that they will always attempt to explain natural phenomena by invoking a deity instead of a modern, scientific explanation that works.

Instead of educating your children with critical thinking skills that enable them to be competent, independent problem solvers, indoctrinate them with the idea that they can find viable solutions to their problems by praying to an imaginary deity who will suspend the known laws of the universe, on their petition, in order to satisfy their perceived needs. After all—ignorant people like you have always invoked a deity to explain the natural phenomena they didn't understand.

When your educationally handicapped children fail to qualify for the final examinations in the competitive 21st century, you can point your finger at the schools and the teachers and blame them for the inadequacies of your children. Keep firmly in mind that YOU are your child's principle teacher. The teachers in the school have a role to play in your child's education, but it is never more than secondary. True education pays incalculably rich dividends; monolithic religious indoctrination extracts a terrible price.

This is a no-holds-barred, tough-love letter by a career science teacher who loved his students and loved his academic discipline. It is also a wake up call to all of the parents who have been victimized by their cultural virus of choice called religion. Please recognize and accept the reality that your children are living in the twenty first century which is a cultural quantum leap beyond the twentieth century that were your formative years. The last half of the twentieth century was a cultural and technological shock that many people could hardly comprehend. The twenty first century shows signs of being another cultural and technological leap that will stagger our collective imagination. We have only just begun.

Your children will be growing up in a society and culture that is so different from the culture you grew up in that by the end of this century you might have a difficult time recognizing it—albeit you won't be alive to see it, but your children and grandchildren might be alive—maybe.

Ancient and archaic world views, like your religion, perpetuated and promulgated by ideological clerics, are so at odds with a modern, scientific understanding of the world's knowledge base that they are like millstones hanging on the necks of your children. Any world view that is to be of value to its adherents must be able to serve as a paradigm for both understanding and explaining the natural phenomena of the world and the cosmos. Since your religion has not and cannot satisfy this intellectual mandate, it is hopelessly and terminally obsolete for your children in the twenty-first century.

Whether you agree with this message, or not, your children will have to acquire the skills necessary to adapt to the realities of the highly competitive twenty first century or they will suffer the consequences. The necessary skills your children require can be obtained in a secular, rigorously academic setting. Those necessary skills and knowledge base cannot and will not be found in any kind of religious indoctrination.

The most important thing you can do for your children is to provide them with a rationale and a scientific paradigm for truth seeking, and then let them fly away on the wings of truth.

Some Thoughts by a Scientist on Faith and Religion While Working in My Garden

Since we, as human beings, are a part of the natural biota of the earth, and the earth is a part of the natural universe, the only thing we can really know about is the natural universe. Therefore Nature is the only thing we can think or talk about. To think or talk about things that are not about Nature is to think or talk about things about which we know nothing. Extra natural (or as some would say, supernatural) things are things about which we know nothing. Therefore, we cannot escape the conclusion that those theologians, priests, pastors and ministers who speak of extra natural (supernatural) things do not know what they are talking about. If we pay any attention at all to people who don't know what they are talking about, what does that say about us?

~~~~~~~~~~~~~~~~~

Considering the magnitude of the universe and its utter indifference to our plight and even existence, and the fact that our sun and all of its attendant planets could disappear in a puff of dust without causing so much as a ripple even in our galaxy, much less the universe at large, it becomes an expression of unimaginable arrogance and unfathomable anthropocentric conceit to place credibility and authority in the claims and assertions of a small tribe of middle eastern pastoralists of about 3000 years ago that their chosen deity was the creator of it all.

~~~~~~~~~~~~~~~~~

If we give assent to a religion that denigrates, disparages and deprecates doubt and skepticism, we close the door to experimentation and inquiry. What then happens to our search for new knowledge?

~~~~~~~~~~~~~~~~~~~

Skepticism, freedom of inquiry and expression, rigorous rational debate and continual challenges to authority are the life blood of democracy and modern life, but anathema to organized religions. Historically, religions could be successful only when they stamped out all dissent. We call this totalitarianism.

~~~~~~~~~~~~~~~~~~~

If we hold that our ethical and moral standards are founded upon unassailable and immutable authority (faith) that originated several thousand years ago in an alien tribal culture, we are at the same time declaring as useless all that we have learned about ourselves and the universe since that time. Is this wise?

~~~~~~~~~~~~~~~~~~~

If we cannot explain natural phenomena, we will be as estranged from the cosmos just as much as were the Neanderthals. Where shall we find answers to our questions about these phenomena? We have historically looked for answers from religion—from the Bible, and the answers have proven to be wrong in every instance. Now we have science as a source of reliable and dependable answers. We shall have to make a choice.

~~~~~~~~~~~~~~~~~~~

Most people are loathe to get involved in a critical discussion on the merits of what they believe is "God." This is because they know intuitively that such a critical examination of their beliefs will show that their beliefs about "God" inevitably collapse into a muddled, confused agglomeration of absurdities and incongruities that is utterly defenseless.

~~~~~~~~~~~~~~~~~~~~

As human beings we have no knowledge except that obtained through our senses and our experience. No one has ever been able to demonstrate that there is any knowledge other than our own. Since we have no knowledge about the design or construction of the cosmos, we have neither authority nor reason to assume a cosmic designer. Using the idea of a cosmic designer to explain the natural phenomena they did not understand is the modus operandi of ignorant savages.

~~~~~~~~~~~~~~~~~~~~

Theological thinking, including all of its attendant intellectual errors, has perverted and corrupted the development of the cognitive processes of children for the last 3000 years. While teachers have a big task dealing with the tabula rasa (blank slate) minds of children, retrofitting their corrupted brains to become critical thinkers instead of "blind believers" is an extremely difficult task. When our educational process does not produce the desired results, we blame the teachers and the schools and fail utterly to understand why students fail to perform as expected.

~~~~~~~~~~~~~~~~~~~~

The progress and development of our society and culture is dependent on our ability to perceive as clearly as possible the world and the cosmos as it is, rather than through the dense fog of theological myths, no matter how attractive they seem to be. Science, not religion, can provide us with reliable answers to our questions about the physical and the factual. The intellectual desert produced by the hallucinogens of religion is the greatest impediment to our comprehension and evaluation of natural phenomena.

~~~~~~~~~~~~~~~~

To imagine a deity from a Biblical context in the light of our modern understanding of the cosmos would be to imagine a god in a way that would be so trite, so limited, so shallow and so poorly understood as to be beneath the dignity and intellect of modern, educated people.

~~~~~~~~~~~~~~~~

Faith is unwarranted conviction in unjustified assertions: e.g. the Bible was inspired by a deity, we will be reunited with loved ones after we die, the creator of the universe hears our prayers, we can conquer disease in our bodies with prayer.

~~~~~~~~~~~~~~~~

Faith is a collection of narratives that we use to explain ourselves whether they are well reasoned or not.

~~~~~~~~~~~~~~~~

Faith absolves one from taking responsibility for one's self.

~~~~~~~~~~~~~~~~

True spirituality is honest emotion hand in hand with reason.

~~~~~~~~~~~~~~~~

People who pray abandon their "thinker" in preference to their "feeler."

~~~~~~~~~~~~~~~~~~~

The great faults of revealed religions are that they are prone to absolutism, extremism, xenophobia, intolerance, divisiveness, persecution, injustice and violence.

~~~~~~~~~~~~~~~~~~~

If any one ever asks you if you believe in god, ask them, "Which one?" Men have invented thousands of gods. If you don't believe in their god, you only believe in one less god than they do.

~~~~~~~~~~~~~~~~~~~

People who attempt to establish truth in their lives with faith can believe in anything, no matter how irrational or illogical or absurd and they can justify any behavior, including murder and genocide.

~~~~~~~~~~~~~~~~~~~

Beliefs that are contrary to the laws of Nature are wrong, no matter who advocates them.

~~~~~~~~~~~~~~~~~~~

When people tell you that they are members of the community of faith, you can tell them that you are a member of the community of reason. Then you can discuss the relative merits of each.

~~~~~~~~~~~~~~~~~~~

An open, flexible, and adaptive mind cannot endorse absolutist ideas.

~~~~~~~~~~~~~~~~~~~

Church Sunday schools do not educate children; they indoctrinate them.

~~~~~~~~~~~~~~~~

"Supernatural" is a one word oxymoron.

~~~~~~~~~~~~~~~~

Heresy exists only in the mind of those who would insist on superimposing their will on you.

~~~~~~~~~~~~~~~~

When you start praying, you have stopped thinking. When you have stopped thinking you have abrogated your humanity.

~~~~~~~~~~~~~~~~

Science seeks answers from nature. Religion imposes answers on nature.

~~~~~~~~~~~~~~~~

Søren Kierkegaard, the Danish philosopher, accepted the virgin birth and bodily resurrection of Jesus as historical fact. He was also known for his neurotic temperament and his convoluted writing style. He wrote, "Religious faith is a pure leap of will uncontaminated by reason or empirical knowledge." I find it impossible to respect that kind of corrupted thinking.

~~~~~~~~~~~~~~~~

The problem with faith is that it doesn't have any cognitive support.

~~~~~~~~~~~~~~~~~~

A pagan is someone who is neither Christian, Jew, nor Muslim whose primary spiritual relationship is with nature and the earth. I must be a pagan.

~~~~~~~~~~~~~~~~~~

There are always more people in church than want to be there.

~~~~~~~~~~~~~~~~~~

We protect ourselves with reason and logic—not magic, faith or superstition.

~~~~~~~~~~~~~~~~~~

The Lord is your Shepherd—if you have the mind of a sheep.

~~~~~~~~~~~~~~~~~~

Any religion based on faith is a kind of philosophical rigidity that retards the development and advancement of our culture.

~~~~~~~~~~~~~~~~~~

The greatest challenge to the human intellect is the recognition and mastery of reality.

~~~~~~~~~~~~~~~~~~

The commands of an unreal deity are in reality only the commands of the priesthood.

~~~~~~~~~~~~~~~~~~

Worship of a deity is a no-brainer ritual.

~~~~~~~~~~~~~~~~~

Religious faith is the triumph of willful, resentful, invincible ignorance over joyful, rewarding, productive intellectualism.

~~~~~~~~~~~~~~~~~

The universe does not make concessions to either ignorance or stupidity.

~~~~~~~~~~~~~~~~~

Science and religion are conceptual lenses for seeking the truth. Both are an attempt to explain and understand our relationship with nature. After acquiring an in-depth understanding of both, one can make an informed decision as to which serves one's best interests.

~~~~~~~~~~~~~~~~~

No god could reasonably expect any intelligent, rational person to take his/her existence on faith.

~~~~~~~~~~~~~~~~~

What sensible reason could any god have for making his/her existence controversial?

~~~~~~~~~~~~~~~~~

Truly good people are good without thought of reward or penalty either here or hereafter.

~~~~~~~~~~~~~~~~~

Religion rejects reason and logic and replaces it with doctrine, dogma and blind faith.

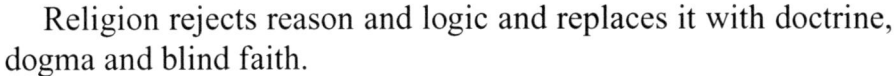

Once you have accepted faith as a valid intellectual premise, you have become a mindless drone without any connection to reality.

~~~~~~~~~~~~~~~~

When religious faith replaces logic and reason, people are prone to criminal behavior.

~~~~~~~~~~~~~~~~

The only solid, truthful basis for morality is reason.

~~~~~~~~~~~~~~~~

Nature is objective and nature is knowable. This is the realm of science. Gods are subjective and unknowable. This is the realm of religion.

~~~~~~~~~~~~~~~~

Instead of healing people, the church paralyzes people's will. Instead of inspiring people, it impoverishes their spirits; instead of freeing people's minds, the church enslaves them with ritual, dogma, and doctrine.

~~~~~~~~~~~~~~~~

While not demanding compelling evidence nor reproducibility nor confirmation nor verification of any kind, religious faith is the original no brainer.

~~~~~~~~~~~~~~~~~~

Unreasoning faith preempts the normal function of the frontal lobe of the human cerebrum.

~~~~~~~~~~~~~~~~~~

Given the ability of the human brain to think rationally, the blind faith of revealed religions is the negation of our humanity and is therefore immoral.

~~~~~~~~~~~~~~~~~~

Gods are the ultimate subjectivities.

~~~~~~~~~~~~~~~~~~

Gods were invented by the more imaginative to instill fear in those who were less imaginative, who might otherwise behave in an evil way.

~~~~~~~~~~~~~~~~~~

In historical retrospect, monotheistic religions with their egregious philosophical and cosmological errors are the worst ideas that have ever happened to the growth and development of Western Civilization.

~~~~~~~~~~~~~~~~~~

Nature is an impersonal phenomenon whose laws of chance and necessity are indifferent to human affairs. The world is constituted of observable matter, not invisible deities. If our lives are sacred, it is because we deem it so, not because imaginary gods created in our own image decided so independent of human thought.

~~~~~~~~~~~~~~~~~~

God is Man's idealization of himself, a kind of anthropomorphic projection, that exists only in the minds of those who find it expedient for their conceived needs.

~~~~~~~~~~~~~~~~~~

Gods and religion are subjective speculation, comfortable illusion, and the denial of reason and reality. Are they then real?

~~~~~~~~~~~~~~~~~~

Religion springs from ignorance of nature and is an attempt to explain nature in the absence of empirical evidence. The intelligent application of evidence renders religion unnecessary as an explanatory construct and is without merit for educated, thinking people.

~~~~~~~~~~~~~~~~~~

We have yet to find a theological explanation for a natural phenomenon that could stand up under the light of critical examination.

~~~~~~~~~~~~~~~~~~

Since no one is born with a particular religious belief, then particular religious beliefs are the product of cultural customs. It follows then that no particular religious beliefs are any more valid than any other, since all are derived from the human experience of one's culture.

~~~~~~~~~~~~~~~~~~

Creativity is stifled when institutions (such as religions) demand or encourage people to accept dogmatically revealed doctrines on faith.

~~~~~~~~~~~~~~~~~

The "Lumen Intellectus Agentis," light of the active intellect, is a natural phenomenon of the human cerebrum and does not require the burden of any theological explanation.

~~~~~~~~~~~~~~~~~

Religious fundamentalism is an exercise in cognitive futility.

~~~~~~~~~~~~~~~~~

Would you renounce your intellectual integrity to preserve your dream of heaven?

~~~~~~~~~~~~~~~~~

Any meaningful search for truth must be tolerant and accepting of pluralism, paradox, irony, and ambiguity. The result will be knowledge that will be fallible and relative, not certain or absolute. This is antithetical to any revealed religion.

~~~~~~~~~~~~~~~~~

Religionists conceive of nature as they want it to be; scientists perceive of nature as it is.

~~~~~~~~~~~~~~~~~

Revealed, theological mystery religions have no more relevance in our attempt to understand our world, the cosmos or the human condition than the Easter Bunny, Santa Claus or Mother Goose.

~~~~~~~~~~~~~~~~~~~~

In spite of the fact that on close examination religious fundamentalism is internally incoherent, logically flawed, philosophically bankrupt and intellectually indefensible, it is still an attractive palliative to the ignorant, the naive and the credulous.

~~~~~~~~~~~~~~~~~~~~

Shielding pet ideas from criticism may be common practice in religion, but it is bad thinking and consequently bad science.

~~~~~~~~~~~~~~~~~~~~

We should always view any assertion or claim that comes with tactics for self protection with extreme skepticism and we should demand the most rigorous scrutiny.

~~~~~~~~~~~~~~~~~~~~

With all of the intellectual rigor of which we are capable, we demand hard, compelling, convincing evidence for reliable truth from our sciences, our system of jurisprudence, our business and commerce, and our educational processes. Why then do most people seem to accept as truth the theological claims and assertions that can not be confirmed, nor verified, nor falsified? It seems that people are prone to imagining that there are regularities where none exist and deny the existence of regularities that they find uncomfortable or unpleasant.

~~~~~~~~~~~~~~~~~~~~

Since there have been, and are, thousands of gods even in recorded history, gods can be understood only in a generic context. For monotheists, i.e., Muslims, Jews or Christians, to suggest or demand that there is only one true god, (theirs), is a statement born of gross ignorance and/or a kind of cultural arrogance that has its roots in tribal xenophobia that is the source of the intolerance that produces the hatred and bigotry that is the source of the violence that thinking people deplore.

~~~~~~~~~~~~~~~~~

Would any one seriously contend that we, the people of the world, with the accumulated wisdom and knowledge of our collective cultures of the last 2000 years have any need whatsoever for an ancient and archaic tome conceived in relative ignorance and composed by religious zealots to find a code of morality and ethics that is appropriate for us in our time? I don't think so.

~~~~~~~~~~~~~~~~~

The difference between scientists and religionists is that scientists seek truth, and religionists believe that they possess the truth.

~~~~~~~~~~~~~~~~~

Religion provides the mind with an escape from guilt.

~~~~~~~~~~~~~~~~~

The failure to adjust to new realities is called stupidity. Religious fundamentalists and others who are in denial of the new realities discovered and endorsed by the world scientific community (e.g. organic evolution) need to get a grip and get up to speed if they are going to be functional in the 21st century. Intellectual self destruction born of ignorance, compounded with stupidity and exacerbated with irrational religious zealotry will not serve their best interests, or those of our society at large.

~~~~~~~~~~~~~~~~~

Judge claims and assertions by the tests of evidence, reason, and logic; not by faith or popular acclaim.

~~~~~~~~~~~~~~~~~~

When religious faith rises, thinking sinks.

~~~~~~~~~~~~~~~~~~

Religion is the accumulation of the sanctification of explanations made by charismatic individuals in an attempt to explain natural phenomena that they did not understand. Modern science uses a different method to explain the realities of the cosmos. The cultural clash has yet to be resolved.

~~~~~~~~~~~~~~~~~~

Religious faith is belief that doesn't rest on reason, logical proof, or material evidence. Does this work for you?

~~~~~~~~~~~~~~~~~~

Living by faith refers to a mode of life that relies on unjustified or false convictions.

~~~~~~~~~~~~~~~~~~

The greatest and grandest and most comfortable illusion of all time, that one can transcend the death of one's body and spend eternity in a blissful existence in a place called heaven is at the same time the cruelest hoax ever perpetrated on humankind.

~~~~~~~~~~~~~~~~~~

When we accept theology, we deny reason. When we deny reason we deny our humanity.

~~~~~~~~~~~~~~~~~~~~

Theology is an edifice in the air, supported by sky hooks, promulgated by charlatans, believed by the ignorant, the naive, and the credulous, that cannot be supported nor verified by either evidence or reason.

~~~~~~~~~~~~~~~~~~~~

Acceptance of theological claims and assertions as valid truth is as risky as trying to jump a chasm with two leaps.

~~~~~~~~~~~~~~~~~~~~

Gods are the ultimate subjectivity, and subjective certainty is an oxymoron.

~~~~~~~~~~~~~~~~~~~~

Religion is pure subjectivity and rules out the objectivity necessary to govern one's life intelligently. We must learn to understand nature as it is, not as we want it to be.

~~~~~~~~~~~~~~~~~~~~

I asked some of my theistically believing friends if their god was a fact or a myth since it had to be one or the other. The first observation of their behavior was that they were ill at ease. If they said god was a fact I would demand that they demonstrate that that was true since facts are demonstrably true. They couldn't do that. If they replied that their god was a myth then they were forced to admit that myths were the products of human imagination, and gods are created in the minds of people. Some thought I had trapped them. Maybe I did, but it surely made them think.

~~~~~~~~~~~~~~~~~~~~

Some have asked, "Does God exist?" I say that if you have to ask, then you obviously have no way of demonstrating that God exists and your question is pointless.

~~~~~~~~~~~~~~~~~

Scientific "truths" are tentative and provisional, but still provide a degree of certainty that works. Religious "truths" provide only certitude that more often than not fails to satisfy our need for what works.

~~~~~~~~~~~~~~~~~

The doctrinal and dogmatic nature of religion is antithetical to the work of scientific discovery; it discourages innovative thinking in our search for new truths.

~~~~~~~~~~~~~~~~~

If God created humankind in his own image, did he represent himself with dignity?

~~~~~~~~~~~~~~~~~

Those people who act selflessly without regard to reward or punishment are the world's most moral people.

~~~~~~~~~~~~~~~~~

The Bible should be understood, analyzed and critically evaluated and then accepted or rejected as a human creation, not as a divine revelation.

~~~~~~~~~~~~~~~~~

The efficacy of the religious scheme of things in monotheistic religions depends upon their exemption from all of the laws of nature. Should this give one cause for pause?

~~~~~~~~~~~~~~~~~~

The god hypothesis is only one of several hypotheses to account for and explain the phenomena of the world, including human destiny. Considering the present level and state of scientifically validated knowledge, the god hypothesis no longer serves the best interests of humankind.

~~~~~~~~~~~~~~~~~~

Religious assertions that are not testable, verifiable or falsifiable and for which there is no compelling evidence must be considered as without intellectual merit by thinking people.

~~~~~~~~~~~~~~~~~~

Religions are a prime source of intellectual segregation and intolerance of diversity.

~~~~~~~~~~~~~~~~~~

If faith is acting on a nobler hypothesis, the nobler hypothesis can never contain untestable, unverifiable or unfalsifiable assertions.

~~~~~~~~~~~~~~~~~~

If one's religious views have the merits that its adherents claim for them, then nothing from the scientific disciplines can possibly make any difference. On the other hand, if the advances of science cast doubt on religious dogma, then maybe a more rigorous examination of the dogma is well advised.

~~~~~~~~~~~~~~~~~~

If the ancient Hebrew cosmology was so weak that they didn't even know the earth was a sphere, can we really justify placing any credibility in the rest?

~~~~~~~~~~~~~~~~~~

In all of history there have been only two ways of understanding and explaining natural phenomena: religion based on faith and revelation neither of which requires evidence, reason, or verifiability; and science which is predicated on evidence, reason and verifiability. Since religion and science are mutually exclusive realms of thought, we shall have to make a choice as to which provides the higher level of veracity.

~~~~~~~~~~~~~~~~~~

Because religions have their roots in fear, ignorance, and superstition, they fail critical intellectual examination; it is precisely why they are antihuman.

~~~~~~~~~~~~~~~~~~

The worship of an imaginary deity from any religion is but an act of gross ignorance commuted in vain selfishness.

~~~~~~~~~~~~~~~~~~

When wishful thinking, warm fuzzy feelings, and subjective speculations are raised to the level of objective fact, we witness the reality of superstition. Religionists would do well to reexamine what they believe is true.

~~~~~~~~~~~~~~~~~~

Organized religions are an intellectual quagmire of attractive, palliative illusions, and praying is the perpetuation of willful ignorance. It is time for all humans to grow and mature enough to put these intellectual traps behind them.

~~~~~~~~~~~~~~~~~~~

In view of the fact that no one has ever presented any credible evidence for the existence of any transcendent deity, and no one has ever presented a credible or cogent argument to justify a deity of any kind, we must conclude that those who argue for a deity must have antecedent psychological motives for such a belief.

~~~~~~~~~~~~~~~~~~~

When religion confines itself to its own domain of meaning, purpose and values, it gets little if any heat from its critics. When religion trespasses into the domain of the physical and the factual, it loses credibility and sacrifices authority in the minds of thinking people. The advances of the sciences have forced religion to retreat from every claim it has made about the natural world. Truly, a Creator God is an idea whose time has passed for educated, reflective thinkers.

~~~~~~~~~~~~~~~~~~~

The intransigent conservatism of religious fundamentalists is indicative of a world view in its death throes. The denial and self delusion of fundamentalists is both an intellectual tragedy and a social disaster.

~~~~~~~~~~~~~~~~~~~

Let us not lose sight of the fact that breaking any of the Biblical ten commandments warrants a penalty of death by either stoning or strangulation according to "The Word of God." Are these penalties consistent with contemporary community standards?

~~~~~~~~~~~~~~~~~

The pseudo sciences of astrology, phrenology, alchemy and palmistry have all been relegated to the trash heap of human cultural advance because the evidence will not support their claims or assertions. The claims and assertions of revealed religions have no more intellectual justification than the pseudo sciences, yet people continue to cling to the comfortable illusions of revealed religions because comfortable illusions are easy and convenient, and reality can be painful and difficult.

~~~~~~~~~~~~~~~~~

Unreasoning faith preempts the normal functioning of the cortex of the prefrontal lobe of the human cerebrum.

~~~~~~~~~~~~~~~~~

Given the unique ability of the human brain to think critically, the blind faith of revealed religions is the negation of our humanity and is therefore immoral.

~~~~~~~~~~~~~~~~~

"End Times", is not the theory of the educated; it is the hypothesis of the ignorant.

~~~~~~~~~~~~~~~~~

In an historical retrospect, monotheistic religions with their philosophical and cosmological errors are the worst ideas that have ever happened to the growth and development of Western civilization.

~~~~~~~~~~~~~~~~~

Gods are the archetypal perfection of human creative thought.

~~~~~~~~~~~~~~~~~

Religion is an attempt to substitute subjective and irrational answers to explain an objective and rational universe.

~~~~~~~~~~~~~~~~~

The Bible lacks internal continuity, historical coherence, and factual veracity. How, then, are we to make meaningful use of it to our purpose?

~~~~~~~~~~~~~~~~~

Much of the Bible is little more than the fictive habits of psychological, ideological and sometimes pragmatic convenience. This is another way of saying it contains a lot of warm, fuzzy illusions. This gives us reason to reflect.

~~~~~~~~~~~~~~~~~

Religious faith is conviction without reason.

~~~~~~~~~~~~~~~~~

Much of religion is the accumulation and sanctification of explanations made by charismatic individuals for the masses in an attempt to explain natural phenomena that they did not understand. Modern science uses a different method to define reality. This has produced a culture clash that has yet to be resolved.

~~~~~~~~~~~~~~~~~

Only convictions that are derived from the human senses or reason can be justified as knowledge; other convictions deserve only the name of belief, or faith.

~~~~~~~~~~~~~~~~~~

Encouraging people to believe in ideas or stories that are known to be untrue (virgin births, resurrections from the dead) has more negative than positive consequences for both individuals and society.

~~~~~~~~~~~~~~~~~~

The displacement of faith and superstition by science and reason has brought real hope to millions who suffer from scores of afflictions and diseases.

~~~~~~~~~~~~~~~~~~

Faith inexorably leads people to unrealistic expectations about their lives and diverts them from accepting responsibility for their own health.

~~~~~~~~~~~~~~~~~~

To pray is to ask or expect that all of the known laws of the universe be suspended or revoked in order that an imagined, beneficent, patriarchal deity satisfy our personal and selfish wants and desires. The arrogance and foolishness of such an act defies understanding.

~~~~~~~~~~~~~~~~~~

The discovery and elucidation of the structure of the DNA molecule by Watson and Crick leaves no room for any theistic or vitalistic account of life that so many people have found so convenient and comfortable for so long.

~~~~~~~~~~~~~~~~~~~

The acceptance of the idea of a system of rewards or punishment by a cosmic judge for our deeds or misdeeds is a measure of the naiveté, gullibility and ignorance of those who subscribe to such unmitigated nonsense.

~~~~~~~~~~~~~~~~~~~

People are unhappy because they are ignorant. Exacerbating their problem is an enigmatic, ineffable, incomprehensible deity who has not offered us any answers to our questions about the natural phenomena of the world in which we live We had to find those answers ourselves. God was no help.

~~~~~~~~~~~~~~~~~~~

When one is ignorant about nature, one can explain all natural phenomena as an act of a deity. Do we then have a better understanding of Nature?

~~~~~~~~~~~~~~~~~~~

Is God a fact, or is God a myth? Is God real, or is God imaginary? If God is a fact and real, then God's existence can be demonstrated. If God's existence cannot be demonstrated, then God is imaginary, unreal and a myth.

~~~~~~~~~~~~~~~~~~~

The doctrinal and dogmatic nature of religion is antithetical to the work of discovery; it discourages innovative thinking in our search for new truths.

~~~~~~~~~~~~~~~~~~~

The Bible should be understood and appreciated as a human creation; not as a divine revelation. If it is a human creation, then it is easily dismissed as an ancient and archaic Hebrew religious myth that has little relevance for us in our time.

~~~~~~~~~~~~~~~~~~~

The efficacy of the religious scheme of things in monotheistic religions depends on their exemption from all of the known laws of the universe. Will this serve our collective best interests?

~~~~~~~~~~~~~~~~~~~

The ideas born of intellectual elitism, though profound, are always delayed as an influence in the thinking of the masses.

~~~~~~~~~~~~~~~~~~~

Any power structure, even that within a church, that discourages or is unreceptive to challenges falls into intellectual sterility and stagnation. This has been the history of revealed religions. That dissent and controversy are necessary elements of intellectual growth seems to have escaped them. We are all the poorer for it.

~~~~~~~~~~~~~~~~~~~

Religions are the source of intellectual segregation and the result is collective ignorance.

~~~~~~~~~~~~~~~~~~~

"In the beginning God created the heavens and the earth." (Genesis 1:1) This is the way ignorance explains what it does not understand. Now, we have science to provide natural answers to our questions about natural phenomena, yet we still have millions of people who cling to supernatural explanations, i.e., "God did it." Is this archaic and obsolete way of thinking still being taught to our children? The advance of modern, creative, humanistic, scientific knowledge and reason has greatly diminished fear and ignorance, and at the same time lifted the human spirit. The rigidity of intractable religious faith, dogma, and doctrine have stifled and suppressed the human spirit for centuries. We can only wonder why the latter still persists in our culture.

~~~~~~~~~~~~~~~~~~~

Because religions fail critical, rigorous, intellectual examination is precisely why they are an insult to educated people and therefore antihuman.

~~~~~~~~~~~~~~~~~~~

The worship of an imaginary god from any religion is an act of gross ignorance committed in vain selfishness.

~~~~~~~~~~~~~~~~~~~

Wouldn't it be wiser to construct our belief system from the known and the real, instead of the unknown and the unreal?

~~~~~~~~~~~~~~~~~~~

What we all need is correct understanding. The question before us is: Will this understanding come from believing or knowing? Will it come from religion or science?

~~~~~~~~~~~~~~~~~~~

Religion is an intellectual quagmire of attractive illusions, and praying is the perpetuation of ignorance. Neither is consistent with modern, rational thought.

~~~~~~~~~~~~~~~~~

When we want or need answers to our questions about natural phenomena, we have to make a choice about where to find dependable, realistic answers that satisfy our desires and needs. Historically, when people needed answers, they had only priests and their religion for those answers. Those answers have proven to be not only unreliable, but in most cases egregiously wrong. So much for the archaic but divinely inspired answers written by Hebrew priests several millennia ago. The answers to our questions about natural phenomena that have been derived from modern science have been responsible for the standard of living we enjoy today. It has been scientific veracity, not religious faith, that has increased life expectancy of approximately 47 years a century ago, to approximately 77 years today. Since all living things, including human beings, are a part of the natural phenomena of the world, we would be best advised to seek our answers about what we are and how we came to be from modern science and not from ancient, archaic dogma and doctrine from any source.

~~~~~~~~~~~~~~~~~

Theology is organized, institutionalized and ritualized ignorance perpetuated by those who have a vested interest in controlling and parasitizing small, weak, dependent minds.

~~~~~~~~~~~~~~~~~

An omniscient god knows not only all of the past and present, it also knows all of the future as well. That being the case, the god must know in advance of all the earthquakes, tsunamis, hurricanes, volcanic eruptions and other deadly natural phenomena. If the god does not warn "his children" of the impending disaster, then he is indifferent to the plight of his children or is incapable of warning them. Should we then love and worship this god.

~~~~~~~~~~~~~~~~~~~

To the fundamentalists and others who are in denial of the scientific truths of organic evolution, we can say that a microscope is of no value to those who refuse to open their eyes.

~~~~~~~~~~~~~~~~~~~

Ideas that have proven with time to be attractive, convenient or comfortable, or to have popular appeal or endorsement, are no guarantee of the truth. Virgin births and the resurrection of the dead have been attractive ideas, and have had popular support for millennia. These ideas have been a part of the mythology of scores of cultures for all of human history. Today we know that both ideas are egregiously false.

~~~~~~~~~~~~~~~~~~~

A sense of friendly or hostile forces in nature of a non-human kind and a sense of mystery born of ignorance play a far greater part in the minds of savages than in the minds of civilized and educated people. Since religion is identified with this kind of feeling, we find in our study of history that every step in human development has shown a diminution of mystery religions based on myths of nature that deny and defy all of the known laws of the universe.

~~~~~~~~~~~~~~~~~~~

Is there anyone who can observe the collection of bodies on a crowded beach on a warm summer day and still assert that their favorite deity was responsible for the creation of such diversity, with the hulking masses of obesity, the malformed and other examples of creation run amok that thoroughly refute any claims of quality control and intelligent creative design.

~~~~~~~~~~~~~~~~~~~

If you had a petulant, jealous god who became so angry because some of his willful children had misbehaved that he destroyed the world and the lives of millions, except for a chosen few "good kids," would you continue to love, honor, respect and worship such a god?

~~~~~~~~~~~~~~~~~~

When our comfortable illusions wrought by revealed religions explode like soap bubbles pierced by the darts of science, we must cope with the scary thoughts of uncomfortable reality.

~~~~~~~~~~~~~~~~~~

The status quo mind set of the conservatives is a denial of the evolution that is inherent in nature and is therefore debilitating, resulting in a culture that has come to the end of its progressive development. The result is cultural death.

~~~~~~~~~~~~~~~~~~

Evolutionary fitness is definable only in relation to a given environment. Given that our culture is evolving at a seemingly exponential rate under the influence of the advances of science, it is readily apparent that the conservative religious fundamentalists with their intransigent adherence to archaic dogma and doctrine are on a slippery slope to cultural extinction. The cultural and scientific evolution of our society proceeds apace in spite of the fundamentalists, not because of them.

~~~~~~~~~~~~~~~~~~

The greater the commitment to a failing cause (religious fundamentalism), the greater the denials to reduce the cognitive dissonance of a world view bereft of reason and logic.

242 L. Rodney Sheffer

~~~~~~~~~~~~~~~~~~

Any attempt to establish truth in our lives based on ancient pagan tribal myths is a life lived in the shadows and the dim light of ignorance, hiding from the bright light of modern, scientific reality.

~~~~~~~~~~~~~~~~~~

Some Biblical scholars have characterized the Gospels as a narrative of restrained imagination, rather than historical biographies. To suggest that a human body that had been dead for three days could come back from the dead and walk and talk among the living can hardly be characterized as "restrained." Rather, it is an imagination run amok in an attempt to create in the mind of a believer a hero figure of superhuman characteristics. However, hero figures of created myths, whether written or oral, who arose from the dead were an old and oft repeated tale at the time the Gospels were written. If Jesus did not arise from the dead, then he would have been a hero figure of lesser stature and magnitude than those who preceded him. Hence, the necessity of Jesus' resurrection from the dead was predicated and dictated by the history of earlier mythical pagan hero figures. Perpetrators, perpetuators and promulgators of religious myths can only sell such ideas as history to the ignorant and the credulous.

~~~~~~~~~~~~~~~~~~

In all of known human history there is no equal to the arrogance, oppression and hatred of others than that so characteristic of the monotheistic religions.

~~~~~~~~~~~~~~~~~~

Virtually all religions have sunk into a state of intellectual stagnation, a kind of status quo born of their claims of certainty that preclude growth, and consequently are inconsistent with the intellectual appetite for more and newer answers about the world we live in. One could argue that religions are inhumane.

~~~~~~~~~~~~~~~~~~

When religions assert that they possess the truth, they leave no room for growth. Consequently, they are a stultifying influence on the development of human culture.

~~~~~~~~~~~~~~~~~~

At this point in our history we need to make a choice of where we are going, how far we can go, and what methodology we can use to get there. We can choose a clear-eyed vision of science born of liberal intellectual openness, logic and reason, or cling to the ancient Bronze Age superstitions, logical incongruities, the briberies of heaven and hell, the semantic obfuscations, contradictions and inconsistencies of an archaic tome conceived and composed in ignorance of all that human culture has learned and accrued in the last 3000 years. While science and religion are both imperfect human constructs, science has proven to be the most reliable method of truth telling ever devised by humankind. While science has been a unifying influence for all of humankind, religions have been the most divisive influence in all of human history.

~~~~~~~~~~~~~~~~~~

Educated people today reject the premise that a legitimate argument can be constructed from authority from any source.

~~~~~~~~~~~~~~~~~~

The advance of human culture depends on the diversity of opinion and dissent. If this were not true, we would still be living in caves and chipping stone tools. Intellectual ferment produces the creativity that is necessary for the evolution of our society. Religions, very conservative by definition, not only discourage, but also have a long history of suppressing new and innovative ideas, and dissent, oftentimes with deadly effectiveness. The result of this suppression has been not only inhibiting the growth and development of human culture, but it has also been eminently destructive. The solution to the problem is the rejection of organized monotheistic religions and the adoption of a humanistic world view predicated on science, democracy, logic and reason. Will this proposed rejection of religions take place soon? That is not going to happen, but a start must be made, or it will never happen at all.

~~~~~~~~~~~~~~~~~

Religious ritual is the soothing anesthetic of familiarity.

~~~~~~~~~~~~~~~~~

Scores upon scores of human cultures have risen in the past only to decline and disappear. The inescapable question is, "Why did they decline and disappear?" The best available answer seems to be that they were the victims of their own inability to adapt to the changing circumstances of both natural phenomena and/ or extreme reluctance to abandon rigid, dogmatic ideas born of religious certitude. Their conservative mind set and their inability to adequately understand and explain their relationship with nature ultimately resulted in their demise. Now we ask ourselves if our culture can long endure, or will it decline and disappear like so many others. We need to be able to find reliable answers to our questions about our relationship with the natural phenomena of the cosmos. Historically, we have sought our answers from authority, and nearly all of that authority was assumed by and vested in theologians of one stripe or another. The revealed truth from such authority was rarely based on the observation, interpretation, and evaluation of nature, rather it was whatever idea was expedient for the authority figure to sell to either an individual or the masses. It is called revealed truth.

~~~~~~~~~~~~~~~~~~

The intellectual error of many religionists is that they imagine that they can arrive at workable, usable answers to questions that are in the realm of the physical and the factual, intuition and feelings about things. Love, art and charity cannot be quantified, but the physical and the factual must be quantified in order to make sense of the universe.

~~~~~~~~~~~~~~~~~~

The history of argument from authority has been a history of abject intellectual tyranny and failure.

~~~~~~~~~~~~~~~~~~

Science is intellectual sanity. Religion is intellectual insanity. Choosing is easy.

~~~~~~~~~~~~~~~~~~

The historic and traditional method of trying to understand and explain our relationship with nature came from the subjective and speculative religious mind set. In our time the objective, scientific mode of understanding nature has superseded and transcended the religious, subjective mind set.

~~~~~~~~~~~~~~~~~~

Our modern scientific culture is predicated on the objective method of the interpretation and evaluation of reality. Should we give our devotion and allegiance to an archaic mythology conceived in the ignorance, arrogance and oppression of a pastoral Bronze Age tribal culture or to an enlightened, modern, scientific, rational world view that we can distill from the better minds among us?

~~~~~~~~~~~~~~~~~~

Religious faith is an intellectual cop-out. With faith you can excuse or evade the necessity of evaluating evidence. Faith is belief without any corroborating evidence, without any confirmation or verification of any kind. If one finds truth by faith, then one can believe in and justify anything no matter how absurd, irrational or illogical. One can justify murder, war and genocide. All of these things have been done. These acts are called sin. Truth by faith? The words credulous and gullible come to mind.

~~~~~~~~~~~~~~~~~~

People become angry when they realize that their attempts to control events and outcomes are often futile. Angst is the awareness that frightful things may happen if people perceive themselves as powerless to prevent them. Prayer is an emotional response to circumstances that people believe are beyond their intellectual control. People pray for help from whatever imaginary deity from their community pantheon they deem most appropriate to try to satisfy their needs or wants. Most people imagine that a beneficent, patriarchal cosmic arbitrator can and will suspend the laws of the universe on their behalf if they are appropriately worshipful, and beg with enough fervor. Helplessness and feelings of inferiority and inadequacy are the product of ignorance. Gods are the inventions and the crutches of the ignorant. Gods are the products of the fear born of ignorance regardless of other labels or virtues assigned to them. For most people gods are the measure of their desperation, and theology is the measure or their gullibility. Since people create their gods in their own image, and the gods are given such powers as omniscience and omnipotence, the creation of such gods amounts to nothing more than self idolatry which is narcissism of the worst kind.

~~~~~~~~~~~~~~~~~

Religions, especially any of the three monotheistic religions of the world, that guarantee that the adherents of these religions will play a starring role in the unfolding of the world's natural phenomena are hopelessly ignorant, naive, insulting and unworthy of educated, civilized people.

~~~~~~~~~~~~~~~~~

Belief, or faith, is the avowal of a policy. If policies are based on logical, rational assertions that can be verified or confirmed with compelling evidence, then beliefs can have merit. Such beliefs can be employed to advantage in the decision-making process that can benefit everyone. If policies do not or cannot meet the above criteria, then beliefs made from these policies are flawed in such a way and to such an extent that decisions made based on such beliefs are most likely to be against the best interest of everyone. This is why faith-based policies and subsequent beliefs are so prone to disastrous results. Societal and cultural catastrophes occur when ideologies take precedence over, or overrule our reason, logic and critical thinking skills.

~~~~~~~~~~~~~~~~~

In settled societies like agrarian cultures, competing factions soon form. In order to maintain cultural stability, the best way to convince people to accept the dictates of "The Big Man" is to involve them in ritual. When people take part in public social activities, they subordinate their individual desires to the higher moral order of the village. Social or ideological schisms are still possible, but are minimized by the social cohesion of a society stabilized by people's inherent inclination for ritual. The social interplay among people will always shake out those who by virtue of guile, force or intimidation become more powerful than others. Those who are at the top of resultant hierarchies are there at the expense of some others who wind up being the have nots. In order to placate those lower on the social hierarchies, the maintenance of social cohesion and stability is the highest priority for those in power.

~~~~~~~~~~~~~~~~~~~

Leaders (chiefs, priests, shamans, et. al.) are those in charge of ritual. Sacred information (THE WORD) is the easiest to control because it can't be confirmed or falsified or verified. If "The Big Man" or the priest says that he speaks for God, or that God speaks to him, how are people of lesser stature going to prove him wrong? Whenever there is inequality, it is justified by invoking a deity with whom the leader is in communication. Unhappy or disgruntled people are pacified by ritual and sacred justification. Hypnotic, repetitive ritual becomes a narcotic that dulls the critical thinking skills of the repressed masses.

~~~~~~~~~~~~~~~~~~~

We should all regard with extreme skepticism a self-appointed or self-authenticating messenger who demands that we behave in a manner that he/she requires, especially if threats of eternal pain and damnation are the price of noncompliance.

~~~~~~~~~~~~~~~~~~~

If truth is but the content of knowledge, we need to ask ourselves how much has revealed religion contributed to our knowledge base in the last 2000 years? I hope everyone understands that the answer is, nothing! Now, ask ourselves how much has science contributed to our knowledge base in the last 100 years? Everyone should make his/her own answer.

~~~~~~~~~~~~~~~~~~~

How can questioning and challenging revealed religions be negative behavior when the result can be the establishment of reason and rationality?

~~~~~~~~~~~~~~~~~

If revealed religion is the only side of the coin that one examines, how can one ever know what the other side of the coin represents?

~~~~~~~~~~~~~~~~~

Ignorance is always more expensive than education.

~~~~~~~~~~~~~~~~~

If religious fundamentalists are so opposed to the findings and truths of evolutionary biology, why do they seek to use science to justify their creationism?

~~~~~~~~~~~~~~~~~

Lies can only achieve marginal success if they are told by those who carry with them an aura of verisimilitude. This is why the lies of religion are so dangerous.

~~~~~~~~~~~~~~~~~

If the Bible is the word of a loving god, are we to just ignore the horrific genocidal atrocities ordered and committed by this same god?

~~~~~~~~~~~~~~~~~

Since the public world is nearly always built on the lowest common denominator, we can postulate that religion will nearly always be a higher priority with the public than will science. We are the poorer for it.

~~~~~~~~~~~~~~~~~~

Some of my acquaintances have labeled my criticisms of their revealed religion as "negative." In reply I asked, "How can questioning and challenging revealed religions be negative behavior when the result can be the establishment of reason and rationality?" They didn't answer.

~~~~~~~~~~~~~~~~~~

If I cannot detect a god with any of my senses, if the god is inaccessible and unapproachable, if the theologians tell me that their god is incomprehensible and totally ineffable, should I love, honor, obey and worship this god? Surely you jest!

~~~~~~~~~~~~~~~~~~

Theologies succeed not because they are logical or rational, or that they can be defended on intellectual grounds, but because of their emotional appeal and that they are effective in coping with despair and inspiring hope, but deriving hope from falsehoods is a recipe for disaster.

~~~~~~~~~~~~~~~~~~

If revealed "truths" have the merits claimed for them, they would all agree, as they are "truths." Since there is wide disagreement among alleged revealed "truths," we cannot realistically or reliably place credibility in any of them.

~~~~~~~~~~~~~~~~~~

Invoking a deity or other ideas from the supernatural to explain natural phenomena is an idea that died a well deserved death in the 19th century. In spite of the scientific advances in our knowledge base over the last 200 years, there are still millions of people who are so ignorant and so naive that they continue to cling to this intellectual error of convenience. In our scientific culture this kind of ignorance will sooner or later be manifested in public policy. Ignorance is prohibitively expensive.

~~~~~~~~~~~~~~~~~

Given our universal regard of jealousy as socially, culturally and intellectually negative behavior, and as an undesirable and potentially malevolent kind of behavior, we are faced with a question. "Can a god be both "jealous" and "good?" The Judeo-Christian god declares himself as a jealous god. (Exodus 20:2-5) We can also now ask, "Is this a mature, sophisticated and intelligent god, or is jealousy a sign of a being who is immature, unsophisticated and of limited intellectual acumen?" If the more mature, sophisticated and intellectual people among us are above jealousy, would it not be better to emulate them than a jealous god?

~~~~~~~~~~~~~~~~~

We all need to know that few people are real "Truth Seekers." Most people believe whatever is convenient and comfortable for them with little reflective thought about whether it is true or not. This is why they are so easily duped by con men. This is why they are so easily manipulated by those who would exploit them. The priests and their functional analogs come to mind.

~~~~~~~~~~~~~~~~~

How could we possibly reconcile a god who is inaccessible to human reason, who is indescribable, incomprehensible, ineffable and undetectable to human senses with a god who wants us to "know" him, love him, and worship him? How could we "know" and obey a god who is so remote and detached from us? If there is only one true god, wouldn't we all "know" and understand this god in the same context? If there is only one god, would there be such profound differences among people in defining or understanding what or who god is? Would a real god allow him/herself to be so enigmatic that we continually quarrel over what god is? We cannot escape the idea that god is whatever each of us wants god to be. Then don't each of us create our own god in a way that suits our own purpose?

~~~~~~~~~~~~~~~~~~~~

God or gods evolved in the minds of humans as a super parent to help them navigate through the rocky vicissitudes of life. Gods were a tool in the minds of people who were ignorant and could not explain the natural phenomena that they didn't understand. Gods were the loving and beneficent parents who had been lost. Gods were the judges we desired to punish those who oppressed us. Gods were those we could beseech to provide us with the things we deemed necessary to sustain us. God is the unqualified love we so desperately want from others. God is the protection we want from evil people. God is the military genius who will lead us to victory over those who would enslave us and do us harm. God is the savior who will save us from death and give us a life of bliss in a wonderful place forever. God is everything and anything you want your god to be.

~~~~~~~~~~~~~~~~~~~~

Faith is giving assent to the proposition of a doctrine or policy. All doctrines and policies are the products of human imaginations. Therefore, faith-based beliefs are believing in what someone else told you you should believe. The error in this kind of truth seeking is self evident to educated people. Faith-based truth can sanction and label as divinely inspired the most monstrous ideas and result in the worst kind of evil. If we are to minimize evil and violence in our culture, we must first abandon faith as a source of truth. Faith as a source of truth in a culture as complex as ours cannot serve our best interests, either individually or collectively.

~~~~~~~~~~~~~~~~~~

Any notion of god that condemns human beings to an ignoble servitude and an unworthy dependence is incompatible with human dignity.

~~~~~~~~~~~~~~~~~~

If we ascribe human attributes to a god, by definition we have limited the scope and magnitude of our god. Who then can define a god and how can a god be defined without committing blasphemy.

~~~~~~~~~~~~~~~~~~

Resting on the couch of dogma and doctrine is the surest way to guarantee intellectual stagnation.

~~~~~~~~~~~~~~~~~~

Religious fundamentalism can exist only among ignorant people. Eliminating this social and intellectual malignancy can only be accomplished by educating our children in an appropriate manner.

~~~~~~~~~~~~~~~~~~

Politics is the art of gaining control by persuasion and superimposing that control on others. How is religion any different?

~~~~~~~~~~~~~~~~~~

When we create a single perfect god, a god who is the quintessential excellence of all we can imagine, a god who is omniscient, omnipotent and omnibenevolent, who possesses absolute knowledge, who is completely and always honest, who represents the eternal perfect love, who represents the sublime happiness, who is the ultimate truth, and then continuously compare ourselves to this perfect deity, we have set a course for our lives of continuous and unmitigated failure.

~~~~~~~~~~~~~~~~~

"Supernatural factors" neither cause nor create breaks in Nature's uniformity or continuity.

~~~~~~~~~~~~~~~~~

Religion as the enemy of change becomes the enemy of the growth, development and progress of our lives and our culture. The problem with religions is that they are frozen ideologies that people find comfortable as they seek constancy, certainty and predictability in their lives that they view as chaotic and out of sync with the natural order. Every aspect of human life is in a constant state of change, or evolution. This dictates a problematic situation for religions, namely how do they provide constancy, certainty and predictability in a world and society that is changing at a near exponential rate. How can religions provide the emotional comfort of ritual and tradition, and change enough to remain relevant to the lives of contemporary people? When religions can come to grips with the fact that science provides our best answers to our questions about natural phenomena, about the physical and the factual, and that religions have a long history of abject failure in these matters, we can all be a lot more at peace with ourselves and each other.

~~~~~~~~~~~~~~~~~

The role of religion must be self constrained to the domain of ethics and morality, who we are and why we are, our behavior, and how we should lead our lives. Science is constrained to its domain of the physical and the factual of natural phenomena. Science is neither equipped nor prepared nor does it make any pretense of authority about spiritual matters or ethical/moral issues. This is in the realm of philosophy or religion. Much of the problem is that religions must recognize that we as human beings are a part of the physical and the factual of the world. Historically, religion has never been equipped nor prepared to provide us with realistic, workable answers to our questions about natural phenomena. It is not equipped nor prepared to do so now. What we are and how we came to be is in the realm of science, and science can provide us with better answers to these questions than religion can. If salvation is what people want, it cannot be found in the scientific realm, and reliable answers about the physical and the factual cannot be found in religion. No one should expect to find all of their answers to all of their questions from either science or religion because neither is able to provide them all. Religionists must understand what is meant by, "Render unto Caesar that which is Caesar's."

~~~~~~~~~~~~~~~~~

Throughout history there have been men who had a pathological, burning desire to have dominion over others; to control them and dictate to them how they may live their lives. Some satisfied their appetite for power in overt ways and became politicians. Others did it by more subtle and devious means, and became priests.

~~~~~~~~~~~~~~~~~

In view of the advances of modern science and the new truths discovered by science, no religion of any kind will ever be able to claim any legitimate authority about the physical and the factual of the universe. "Who" we are, and "why" we are may be in the realm of religion, but the "what we are", and the "how we came to be" is permanently and exclusively in the realm of science for the rest of our history.

~~~~~~~~~~~~~~~~~~

When people pray, when they beseech and implore their favorite deity for their desires or needs, they are asking that the known laws of the universe be suspended on their behalf. This is the most monstrous and bottomlessly selfish act imaginable. This is so absurd we can only wonder how a reasonably intelligent person can behave in such an ignorant manner. This begs the question: Who has been teaching our children, and what are they being taught?

~~~~~~~~~~~~~~~~~~

In our modern, scientific, high tech culture we continue to cling to archaic religious traditions and modes of thought that have left us ill prepared and dangerously unfit for life in the twenty first century as we plod like lemmings toward destruction assured by conservative religious obsolescence—all the while with a pious, self righteous smile on our faces. It cannot be derived from any external source

~~~~~~~~~~~~~~~~~~

People want and need to have their lives have meaning and purpose. However, as just one of the millions of species of living things that have evolved on this planet, our lives have no more inherent meaning or purpose than an earthworm, or a fungus. Nature does not play favorites and is absolutely unimpressed with our anthropocentric arrogance and claims of being "special." The definition of whatever meaning or purpose our lives are to have is up to us. It cannot be derived from an external source.

~~~~~~~~~~~~~~~~~~~

Since most people do not, or cannot, do a very good job of defining their own importance, meaning or purpose, they are literally trapped in their own ignorance and dependent on someone else to decide and tell them what the meaning or purpose of their life is to be. This is the price these people pay for their ignorance. They are sheep who need a shepherd to follow.

~~~~~~~~~~~~~~~~~~~

If you ask me if I believe in a god that cannot be detected by my senses, I say that your question lacks meaning and is therefore cognitively worthless.

~~~~~~~~~~~~~~~~~~~

When faith and revelation rise, reason and rationality fade away.

~~~~~~~~~~~~~~~~~~~

Ideas about a life after death are rooted in the most primitive kinds of speculation and superstition born of the ignorance of savage and barbaric people. Are you a savage and barbaric person?

~~~~~~~~~~~~~~~~~~~

Religion is the mind-numbing narcotic to which the religious are addicted. What is most needed is the actual understanding of things that is achieved through reason, logic and science. Instead we have the unknowableness of things born of the fear, ignorance and superstition of supernaturalistic religion. It is time for us to grow up intellectually and abandon the dogmatic nonsense of revealed religions.

~~~~~~~~~~~~~~~~~~~

Every religion has at its very foundation a misconception and misinterpretation of natural phenomena, and all worship is based on a belief that some being causes and can change the outcome of these phenomena.

~~~~~~~~~~~~~~~~~~~

There is nothing in this world more dangerous than religious certitude coupled with dedicated conviction. A god or gods are illusions created by people's brains to satisfy a conceived need as they seek to explain and understand their place in the cosmos.

~~~~~~~~~~~~~~~~~~~

The more people invoke deities to explain the vicissitudes in their lives the more ignorant they are. The more educated people become, the less they need to depend on external sources to explain their lives.

~~~~~~~~~~~~~~~~~~~

The Church's concern for human life as embryos does not square with its long history of murdering people who did not agree with its preposterous theology, doctrines and dogma.

~~~~~~~~~~~~~~~~~~~

Religions are the organized, systematized, dogmatized, anthropomorphic projections that have risen from the ignorance of history and nature.

~~~~~~~~~~~~~~~~~~~

The dinosaurs were the dominant form of animal life on earth for one hundred fifty million years. When profound change occurred, they could not evolve and adapt fast enough to avoid extinction. Christianity has been the dominant religion in Western Civilization for nearly two thousand years. In the last hundred years or so, profound changes have occurred that dictate that adaptation to the changes will be necessary if Christianity is to avoid extinction. The factor that has dictated the necessity of change is called "modern science."

~~~~~~~~~~~~~~~~~~

Science is now the prevailing paradigm for assessing, evaluating and explaining the natural phenomena of the world and the cosmos. The objective, the physical and the factual in our lives cannot be adequately addressed or understood by the subjective, ancient and archaic myths that reflect the ignorance, the tribal biases and the superstitions of those who wrote the Bible. The Biblical "miracles" that defy and deny the known laws of the universe can no longer get credible recognition from educated people. Our need to know who we are, and why we are, can remain in the realm of philosophy or religion along with the ethical and moral codes that help us govern how we should lead our lives. However, if we are to make intelligent, informed decisions about our place in the cosmos, what we are and how human beings came to be, can only be adequately answered by our understanding of natural phenomena, as we are a part of the world's natural phenomena. That objective understanding comes only from science.

~~~~~~~~~~~~~~~~~~

Obsolescence is the reality of inevitable change in the history of the world. The history of the dinosaurs is the preeminent lesson for Christians: evolve and adapt to new scientific realities or face extinction.

~~~~~~~~~~~~~~~~~~

People who look to their religion for little more than a set of answers are intellectually paralyzed and in need of enlightenment. A legitimate religion with intellectual merit provides an avenue for seekers who will courageously consider and examine all perspectives. Dogma and doctrine to the exclusion of competing or contrasting ideas results in personal and societal stagnation, and cultural death. Religious fundamentalists, whether Christian or Muslim, who assert that they have the truth to the exclusion of all other ideas are the source of the absolutism, intolerance, and bigotry that gives rise to hatred, persecution, and violence the world over.

~~~~~~~~~~~~~~~~~~

Those who accept the preaching they hear without skeptical and critical examination of the messages perpetuate the ignorance of the preachers by default as they abrogate their birthright as sentient human beings.

~~~~~~~~~~~~~~~~~~

Biblical writers frequently created historical "facts" based on what they wanted on theological grounds. We cannot derive historical fact or an adequate understanding from religious myth.

~~~~~~~~~~~~~~~~~~

Religion attempts to establish credibility about "miracles" with a priori rules. This rules out any subsequent analysis, verification or evaluation of the story. This is not consistent with our ideas of academic honesty or intellectual integrity. Thus, Biblical stories that contradict, deny, and defy the known laws of the universe are totally inconsistent with modern ideas of what is and can be true.

~~~~~~~~~~~~~~~~~~

Man-made dogmas and doctrines derived from faith along with ornate rituals and powerful emotions do not validate the flimsy ideas and irrational premises of revealed religions.

~~~~~~~~~~~~~~~~~~

Reassuring religious beliefs allow people to cope with anticipated misfortune, bad luck, and the vagaries of life, albeit they may be irrational and based on magic, superstition, and ignorance. Such beliefs are the bargain of a loser.

~~~~~~~~~~~~~~~~~~

(With apologies to Ambrose Bierce) Petitionary prayer is nothing more than the pitiful, pathetic and importunate whimperings of the ignorant and the naive as they implore their imaginary deity to suspend the laws of the universe on their selfish behalf. The weak and the powerless beseech their "Big Daddy" in the sky for their perceived needs or desires. For such people nothing has changed in the last 10,000 years, and for people of such meager intellectual acumen nothing will change in the next 10,000 years.

~~~~~~~~~~~~~~~~~~

Gods created by human imagination are the acceptable substitutes for the kind of humans they would like to have watch over them—the idealized parent, especially a powerful, benevolent father who is both provider and protector.

~~~~~~~~~~~~~~~~~~

Most people are inclined to believe based on what they fear more than what they believe based on legitimate knowledge.

~~~~~~~~~~~~~~~~~~

The real, true remedy for all of our problems can be derived from verifiable knowledge, never from unverified dogma.

~~~~~~~~~~~~~~~~~~

People who are adherents to a given religious faith may speak of the pain felt and the angst induced by the attacks on their beliefs, but they pay little mind to the pain and angst they have delivered to those who brought new truths to them.

~~~~~~~~~~~~~~~~~~

Defining what is righteous and what is sinful is possible only by reference to the consequences of a given act. Since acts and consequences are variable, righteousness and sinfulness can only be relative. Can we then govern our lives with absolute, inflexible mandates derived from religious dogma and doctrine?

~~~~~~~~~~~~~~~~~~

Old traditions and established authorities have value in our society because they provide constancy and predictability which bring domestic tran-quility. However, under conditions of social and cultural change, the old traditions and established authorities can lead to obsolete and harmful customs. Thus, we find it prudent to continually question and reevaluate those "Old Traditions" and "Established Authorities" lest we become obsolete.

~~~~~~~~~~~~~~~~~~

It is easy to declare that God is truth, but it is also easy to make an abstract noun "truth" from an adjective "true." Is that helpful?

~~~~~~~~~~~~~~~~~~

To imagine or assert that the biological world is the product of Divine Design that corresponds to eternal law is an act of gross ignorance of the biological world which includes human beings. The inconsistencies, incongruities, and nonsensical products of the evolutionary process are totally at odds with the objectives of a Divine Designer. As an indeterminate process, evolution cannot be the product of an omniscient creator god. There is no evidence of intention of a deity in the biological world.

~~~~~~~~~~~~~~~~~

Even intelligent, educated people will behave irrationally in defense of a cherished irrational belief.

~~~~~~~~~~~~~~~~~

Beliefs based on emotion and faith are those that most often lead to dreadful consequences.

~~~~~~~~~~~~~~~~~

A perfect recipe for social disaster consists of equal portions of unbounded passion, conscientious stupidity, total commitment, willful ignorance and blind faith. Doesn't this sound like a religious proselytizer?

~~~~~~~~~~~~~~~~~

Science teaches people to doubt, and religion teaches people to believe. Science places value on skepticism, religion on gullibility. We can choose.

~~~~~~~~~~~~~~~~~

Theology is a gossamer web of speculative, subjective abstractions with neither evidentiary support nor logical merit. We are therefore well advised to regard it as cognitively worthless.

~~~~~~~~~~~~~~~~~~

The arguments of religionists more often than not depend on the uncritical acceptance (faith) of imprecise analogies. The results are intellectual errors that preclude our search for truth.

~~~~~~~~~~~~~~~~~~

How could people ever grow up if they are the dependent "Children of God" all of their lives?

~~~~~~~~~~~~~~~~~~

The tendentious fictions of the Bible proffered by zealous priests as the "Word of God" apparently don't require much salesmanship to ignorant, credulous people. We need to be very careful about what we accept on faith as "truth".

~~~~~~~~~~~~~~~~~~

Certainly there is an element of subjective/intuitive thinking and leaps of imagination in the creative aspect of the scientific enterprise. However, we must keep in mind that before the discoveries of science become a part of our common knowledge base, the findings of science are rigorously examined and scrutinized by skeptics and repeated, objective verification and confirmation are required before we accept the findings as scientific truth. Can we say the same for the assertions of revealed religions?

~~~~~~~~~~~~~~~~~~

Blind faith in and unquestioning love for one's parent either real or imagined is childish thinking.

~~~~~~~~~~~~~~~~

Our most pressing problem in America today is that our legislators are intellectually handicapped by a religious straitjacket of faith that predisposes them to failure as they attempt to deal rationally with the nation's problems.

~~~~~~~~~~~~~~~~

If we give assent to a religion that denigrates, disparages, and deprecates doubt and skepticism, we close the door to experimentation and inquiry. What then happens to our search for new knowledge?

~~~~~~~~~~~~~~~~

If we demand that our legislators believe in a god whose existence cannot be demonstrated, why should we be surprised if they are disingenuous, deceitful and delusional?

~~~~~~~~~~~~~~~~

If we hold that our ethical and moral standards are founded upon un-assailable authority (faith) that originated several thousand years ago in an alien tribal culture, we are at the same time declaring as useless all that we have learned about ourselves and the universe since that time. Is this wise?

~~~~~~~~~~~~~~~~

If the primary focus of our lives is on a deity, then our concern for our fellow human beings can only be secondary. For humanists the primary focus is on improving the lives of other human beings.

~~~~~~~~~~~~~~~~~~~

Theological elaborations superimposed on our attempts to understand and explain natural phenomena succeed only in corrupting and distorting our comprehension of reality.

~~~~~~~~~~~~~~~~~~~

Fundamentalists are in denial of the reality of the world, but the consequences of that denial will never go away.

~~~~~~~~~~~~~~~~~~~

The founders of every religion were in profound disagreement with every extant religion. This is as true today as it was thousands of years ago. Does this give primacy of authority to any one of them?

~~~~~~~~~~~~~~~~~~~

The massive, expensive, ornate and elaborate religious edifices be they churches, temples or cathedrals paid for by poor people are products of priest craft to convince ignorant masses that they (the priests) are the mediators of wisdom, truth and the power between them (the masses) and god. The naive, the credulous, and the ignorant continue to this day to buy into this insidious illusion created by priests.

~~~~~~~~~~~~~~~~~~~

Compared to the mind-boggling accomplishments of science in the last 150 years, religious beliefs seem primitive, archaic, elementary and woefully lacking in innovation or imagination. A need for a higher, more sophisticated level of understanding of the world and the cosmos than religious texts offer seems not only self evident but necessary and prudent.

~~~~~~~~~~~~~~~~~~~

If your knowledge base has the adequate depth and breadth and your critical thinking skills are sufficiently honed, you will recognize the futility of petitionary prayer and have no need of such magical thinking and irrational behavior.

~~~~~~~~~~~~~~~~~~~

Those who come down to the beach in the morning to watch the sun rise out of the sea understand better than anyone else why primitive man made a deity out of the sun.

~~~~~~~~~~~~~~~~~~~

Theistic gods are not so much about cosmic authority or creative talent, but rather they are about people's idealization of themselves and their appetite for power and dominion over others.

~~~~~~~~~~~~~~~~~~~

The Hebrew Bible says that the Hebrews are the chosen people of their Hebrew god. (Isn't that just special?) If only the Hebrews are the chosen elite, then all others of god's children (the Gentiles) must be the unchosen people. They are not rejected people, but certainly those who can never be among the chosen. Gentile Christians then, by definition, can never be more than second class people in the eyes of their Hebrew god. Is this a god for you?

~~~~~~~~~~~~~~~~~~~

Religious superstition combined with passion and commitment can produce a disease that can be cured only by a prescription for a healthy dose of logic, reason, science and critical thinking skills. This prescription can be filled in a good, secular school. It cannot be filled in a church.

~~~~~~~~~~~~~~~~~

The progress and development of our society and culture is dependent on our ability to perceive as clearly as possible the world and the cosmos as it is, rather than through the dense fog of theological myths, no matter how attractive they seem to be. Science, not religion, can provide us with reliable answers to our questions about the physical and the factual. The intellectual desert produced by the hallucinogens of religion is the greatest impediment to our comprehension and evaluation of natural phenomena.

~~~~~~~~~~~~~~~~~

No matter what kind or how much evidence to the contrary, a believer will never abandon a comfortable illusion if it satisfies a deep psychological need.

~~~~~~~~~~~~~~~~~

Truth by faith becomes a palliative only when evidence and reason have not been found to support a claim or assertion.

~~~~~~~~~~~~~~~~~

The fatal flaw in faith as a means of arriving at the truth of a proposition is that faith has no criteria for separating truth from falsehood.

~~~~~~~~~~~~~~~~~

Gods are not only the ultimate subjectivity; they are an unverifiable hypothesis as well. Thus, the subject has little or no cognitive value and consequently is hardly worth our attention or discussion.

~~~~~~~~~~~~~~~~~

Theologians are delusional speculators trapped in a mental miasma of obfuscation and confusion of their own making all the while destined for intellectual extinction. Should we follow their example?

~~~~~~~~~~~~~~~~~

Skepticism, freedom of inquiry and expression, rigorous rational debate and continual challenges to authority are anathema to organized religions. Historically, religions could be successful only when they stamped out all dissent.

~~~~~~~~~~~~~~~~~

The idea of a single male deity is the original sexist statement.

~~~~~~~~~~~~~~~~~

A major part of a person's world view is a strategy for living his/her life. How shall we conduct our lives? Historically, under the rubric of the world's monotheistic religions, the dictate or proscription has been, "Believe and Obey!" For uneducated, non-thinking sheep this may have been the only option. If, however, one is an adequately educated critical thinker, adapting to new knowledge and adopting modern modes of thought would seem to be the more rewarding option.

~~~~~~~~~~~~~~~~~

If the fundamentalists will give only a literal interpretation of their Bible, then their god, the "author", must be incapable of employing metaphor, allegory and symbolism as literary devices.

~~~~~~~~~~~~~~~~~

How else can we explain or characterize belief by faith than as mental negligence or arrested cognitive development?

~~~~~~~~~~~~~~~~~

Religions are the product of ignorance, magical thinking, superstition, and an impoverished imagination. This is why educated people reject them.

~~~~~~~~~~~~~~~~~

You admittedly believe in a god about whom you know nothing, and you think I should behave as irrationally as you in this matter? Surely you jest!

~~~~~~~~~~~~~~~~~

If you are a Christian, Muslim or Jew and disavow all but one of the thousands of gods listed in our libraries, and I disavow all of them, how much different am I than you?

~~~~~~~~~~~~~~~~~

When we consider what is known of the earth and its sister planets, orbiting around our sun—a minor star in a galaxy of 100 billion stars, in a universe of billions of galaxies, we also understand that the cosmogony of the Biblical story of creation is a fanciful, mystical, mythological, allegorical narrative conceived in total ignorance of the reality of the cosmos and other natural phenomena. To realize that people in our scientific age still believe that this is factual history is hard evidence that the promulgators and perpetuators of this misinformation are guilty of intellectual abuse of all of their believers. We have a moral issue here.

~~~~~~~~~~~~~~~~~

The alleged miracles of the Biblical narratives, in the light of modern scientific knowledge of the physical and the factual, make clear that such fanciful stories are the product of barbaric superstition and unmitigated ignorance. Today they are only lies perpetuated by the priesthood, and have no legitimate place in the knowledge base of educated people.

~~~~~~~~~~~~~~~~~

Why should we put any more faith in ancient myths than in our own?

~~~~~~~~~~~~~~~~~

The acceptance of theological explanations for the understanding of natural phenomena is a kind of intellectual and cultural cognitive suicide.

~~~~~~~~~~~~~~~~~

We can be no more supernaturally informed than we can be supernaturally nourished.

~~~~~~~~~~~~~~~~~

Those who are intolerant of the views of others have no right to ask that their views be respected.

~~~~~~~~~~~~~~~~~

The prime requisite for historians is that they must be dispassionate and be detached from their subject. Objectivity and absence of bias is necessary for a historian to have credibility. The Hebrews and Christians who wrote the mystical, mythological, allegorical narratives that make up the Biblical stories did not even try to be detached or objective and without bias as they composed their religious tome. Their intent was to advance a religio-political agenda. Therefore, what they wrote cannot under any circumstances be regarded as what we understand to be historically accurate. Religious zeal and political agendas by the authors of the Bible do not make for historical veracity.

~~~~~~~~~~~~~~~~~~~

For most people, the weakness in their philosophy is that they are inclined to believe as true whatever they find as convenient and comfortable. This is true for politics or religion. This may have a kind of superficial usefulness, but the kind of truths that are needed for an accurate and reliable assessment of reality are available only from a higher and more sophisticated level of thinking. Science comes to mind.

~~~~~~~~~~~~~~~~~~~

Petitionary prayer is the pitiful, pathetic, puerile and importunate whimpering of ignorant people beseeching their favorite deity for relief from the vicissitudes of their lives.

~~~~~~~~~~~~~~~~~~~

Faith is the mother of all doctrine and dogma—both of which shut the door to all new knowledge, critical inquiry and experimentation.

~~~~~~~~~~~~~~~~~~~

Religious faith is how ignorant people use superstition to cope with uncertainty.

~~~~~~~~~~~~~~~~~~~

Today, Islam as it is being practiced, is on the wrong side of history. What Islam needs is what The Enlightenment did to temper Christianity and limit its power. Islam must be reinterpreted by Muslims in a way that guarantees sexual equality, democracy, freedom of expression and personal liberty. Without these necessary changes Islam is doomed to extinction. Will that occur in time?

~~~~~~~~~~~~~~~~~

All religions, like all political ideologies, are the products of the imaginations of ambitious people as they seek dominion and power to influence, direct and control other people.

~~~~~~~~~~~~~~~~~

Institutionalized religion is the corruption of and the antithesis of true spirituality.

~~~~~~~~~~~~~~~~~

The harm that I see in religions in general, and the monotheistic religions in particular, is their need to have absolute truths that are not to be challenged, or even questioned. This effectively shields the believers from any new knowledge or contrary evidence that might challenge the faith. The power of the hierarchy must be maintained at all costs. The result is intellectual tyranny and cultural regression. Also to be considered is that this kind of authoritarianism corrupts the cognitive processing of children. This results in a stunted mind trapped in a kind of intellectual channel that has neither depth nor breadth and fails to recognize the necessity of making conclusions on the evidence instead of archaic dogmas. The open horizon of a child's mind is suffocated by the darkness of a closed mind. Children don't deserve to be treated that way, and society cannot afford this egregious intellectual error.

~~~~~~~~~~~~~~~~~

There is no arrogance quite like the arrogance of religious faith.

~~~~~~~~~~~~~~~~~~

All of the gods from all cultures are mystical, mythological, allegorical narratives except that the Judeo-Christian god is touted by the believers to be the only true god. Their problem is that the evidence to support their assertion and their arguments is not any more compelling than those for the other gods. Are we not justified in composing our own myths, in our own time, to suit our own purposes as those who composed their myths more than 2000 years ago?

~~~~~~~~~~~~~~~~~~

In view of our modern understanding of the cosmos, to imagine a deity in a Biblical context would be to imagine a god in a way that would be so trite, so limited, so shallow and so poorly understood as to be beneath the dignity and intellect of modern, educated people.

~~~~~~~~~~~~~~~~~~

If we give assent to a belief system that can neither be confirmed nor verified, can neither be proven nor disproven, can we criticize those who regard us as gullible or even stupid?

~~~~~~~~~~~~~~~~~~

We are all better off if we seek justification for ideal values from ourselves, here and now, instead of expecting to find them in the remote and transitory. After all, we are individuals with a short personal history. We live only in the here and now. An afterlife is purely illusory.

~~~~~~~~~~~~~~~~~~~

Religion tries to turn thought into the business of finding a simplistic, transcendent remedy for the complex issue of trying to understand and explain natural phenomena. Of course this has never worked, but in this scientific/ technological culture it is futile and hopeless.

~~~~~~~~~~~~~~~~~~~

When people have been lead to believe that they have an absolute truth from an Absolute Authority, they have swung the doors to disaster wide open. Religious certainty borne of absolute truth and coupled with religious conviction is the most dangerous—indeed the most lethal combination in human history. Blaise Pascal wrote, "Men never do evil so completely and cheerfully as when they do it from religious conviction." More people have been persecuted, tortured and killed as a consequence of religious certitude than for any other cause. The Crusades, the Inquisition, the Holocaust, the jihads, the pogroms, the witch hunts and countless other atrocities against humankind were all derived directly from religious absolutism and certainty.

~~~~~~~~~~~~~~~~~~~

Religion is, after all, an a priori explanation of natural phenomena. In contrast science is an a posteriori explanation of natural phenomena. Religion attempts to force nature into an ideological straitjacket to suit its preordained agenda—an attempt to make nature be what it wants it to be. Science, on the other hand, attempts to derive answers to our questions about natural phenomena by observation, interpretation, and evaluation of what nature is, without superimposing any artificial veneer of an extra-natural agenda constructed by priests or their analogs. We need to critically examine the contrast here and decide if one or the other is best suited for our decision-making process.

~~~~~~~~~~~~~~~~~~~~~~

Some "Godists" allege that modern science is nothing more than a latter day religion, and that scientists are the priests attempting to advance a newer agenda of doctrine and dogma of science. This not only cannot be justified, it is false. The assertions of Godists can be neither verified nor confirmed and are supported only by faith. Scientific assertions are and must be supported by compelling evidence and must be verifiable. Therein lies the real difference.

~~~~~~~~~~~~~~~~~~~~~~

Religion may make people comfortable when needs be, but the price they pay for their comfort is an enslaved mind.

~~~~~~~~~~~~~~~~~~~~~~

Both faith and critical thinking are mental modes that people use for deriving their future decisions and actions. The foundation of faith is emotions, and the foundation of critical thinking is our rational intellect. This distinction is worth our consideration.

~~~~~~~~~~~~~~~~~~~~~~

What the clergy and some believers are demanding of people is that they adopt, cling to and defend a static, archaic world view derived from the fear, ignorance, magic, and superstition of an ancient and alien tribal cultural milieu of 2000 to 3000 years ago that has little if any relevance to us in our culture and in our time. Does that seem like a good idea?

~~~~~~~~~~~~~~~~~~~~~~

Any idea, story, dogma or doctrine that is not true, is dangerous especially in the minds of naive, ignorant people.

~~~~~~~~~~~~~~~~~~

People adhere to religious explanations because they are convenient and comfortable. People accept scientific explanations because the evidence, logic, and reason are compelling and convincing.

~~~~~~~~~~~~~~~~~~

In the evolution of human culture, theology is the first, most elementary and most primitive stage for assessing reality. Next comes metaphysics with more subjective speculations and absence of verification of assertions. Last, and most modern comes science, with its empirical support, verification, and self-correcting paradigm. This is worth our consideration.

~~~~~~~~~~~~~~~~~~

Religion should provide us with an acceptable view of humankind. People should understand their humanity in celebratory exultation. Christianity as it has historically been constituted fails this criterion. Perhaps this is why Bishop John Shelby Spong wrote a book entitled Why Christianity Must Change or Die.

~~~~~~~~~~~~~~~~~~

In the search for truth, science starts with questions and seeks answers. Religion starts with answers, and winds up in question.

~~~~~~~~~~~~~~~~~~

Science is evidence without certainty. Religion is certitude without evidence.

~~~~~~~~~~~~~~~~~~

In view of the fact that there are and have been thousands of gods, the term "god" can only be used in a generic context. Any attempt to use the term "god" in a specific context is an affirmation of cultural arrogance compounded by unmitigated ignorance.

~~~~~~~~~~~~~~~~~~~~~~~~

Eternal verities cannot be found in claims or assertions that can neither be tested, verified, nor confirmed and are immune from scrutiny and disproof. Warm, fuzzy lies may be comfortable, but they are still lies.

~~~~~~~~~~~~~~~~~~~~~~~~

Collective guilt (original sin) like collective punishment (Noachian Flood) are archaic ideas that are cognitively worthless and rejected by appropriately educated people.

~~~~~~~~~~~~~~~~~~~~~~~~

The only thing we have acquired from Biblical miracle stories is error.

~~~~~~~~~~~~~~~~~~~~~~~~

Subjective certitudes, like religious faith, can sanction any kind of fanaticism or atrocity.

~~~~~~~~~~~~~~~~~~~~~~~~

Religions thrive on ignorance and perish in the bright light of critical thought.

~~~~~~~~~~~~~~~~~~~~~~~~

Faith is belief that is unverifiable and unsupported by facts. It is a tool used by believers to remake the real world into a "wish world" by projecting their a priori values on it.

~~~~~~~~~~~~~~~~~

When people accept an idea or policy as truth without any confirming or corroborating evidence, we call this "a leap of faith." Truth established by faith means "anything goes." This archaic principle corrupts honest inquiry and skews the data of legitimate research.

~~~~~~~~~~~~~~~~~

Ideologues with their subjective view of reality are always threatened by the objectivity of the empirical—the data. Factual information will always be condemned by those who prefer a priori policy to a posteriori evidence. The convenient and the comfortable will always be preferred by most people to cold, hard reality.

~~~~~~~~~~~~~~~~~

Faith-based initiatives are the sole support for all brands of extremism and absolutism that can ultimately cascade into persecution and violence.

~~~~~~~~~~~~~~~~~

Religious belief is a poorly executed leap into irrationality.

~~~~~~~~~~~~~~~~~

Subjective certitudes, like religious faith, can sanction any kind of fanaticism or atrocity.

~~~~~~~~~~~~~~~~~~

There are two kinds of sin. The first is the things you say or do that are harmful to other people. The second is stupidity or willful ignorance—refusing to learn in the face of new evidence.

~~~~~~~~~~~~~~~~~~

Reason, logic, and critical thinking skills might have confirmed our deities and demons if in fact they were real; instead they have only relegated such absurdities as irrelevant, archaic superstitions.

~~~~~~~~~~~~~~~~~~

The most difficult thing people have to do is to abandon religious certitude about the physical and the factual and to adopt the tentative and provisional truths of science.

~~~~~~~~~~~~~~~~~~

To sophisticated thinkers, deities are nothing more than superstition and archaic, intellectual clutter.

~~~~~~~~~~~~~~~~~~

In the light of our modern knowledge base built on solid science, religious assertions about natural phenomena are obsolete, irrelevant and false.

~~~~~~~~~~~~~~~~~~

Religions provide people with an organized, ritualized and sanctified ideology to justify their natural xenophobic tendency. The "Us vs. Them" hostility can be maintained and justified by claiming a divine sanction: "We are the chosen people of our god." This policy and practice was adaptive for survival in a pre-modern, preliterate, tribal culture, but our modern society has evolved and progressed beyond the point at which this kind of thinking can be tolerated. It is divisive, exclusionary and the prime factor in the formation of intolerant attitudes towards others that breeds the bigotry and hostility that leads so easily to persecution and violence.

~~~~~~~~~~~~~~~~~

Religious faith is intellectual and moral laziness.

~~~~~~~~~~~~~~~~~

If we have intellectually satisfying and demonstrably true modern, scientific answers to our questions about natural phenomena, why would we turn to a subjective, archaic paradigm like religion for those answers?

~~~~~~~~~~~~~~~~~

Has immersing ourselves in a mystical, mythological, theological world of spiritual imaginings and expectations of heavenly interventions provided us with any real solutions to our problems as we cope with the vicissitudes of life on earth? I think not!

~~~~~~~~~~~~~~~~~

Wouldn't an omniscient, omnipotent, omnibenevolent god find a better way to redeem sinful humans than to sacrifice (kill) his only son in such a barbaric way as crucifixion? Would any sane, civilized person do such a thing?

~~~~~~~~~~~~~~~~~

In the realm of religious faith, rationality is abandoned, the established legitimacy of science is ignored or suppressed. We extinguish the sunlight of reason and read our primitive, tribal writings by the candlelight of superstition while we exercise no more discretion upon their literal words than an ignorant, naive child.

~~~~~~~~~~~~~~~~~~

Priest craft, or in a more modern context, Spin Doctoring, is more and more recognized for what it is—a means of controlling the minds and behaviors of the masses of willful people who increasingly are better educated, wiser, and less given to manipulation by the entreaties, scams and threats of priests. Believers think that faith gives intellectual legitimacy to their intellectually indefensible world view. Some of us know better.

~~~~~~~~~~~~~~~~~~

Any religion that is to retain credibility and relevance in the eyes and minds of modern, intelligent people must evolve fast enough to be consistent with a modern knowledge base. Failing this necessary transition at a satisfactory rate, a religion like Christianity or Islam becomes labeled, and deservedly so, as archaic, ancient and consequently obsolete. The cognoscenti of the world, unable to reconcile the Biblical miracles (virgin births and resurrection myths, et. al.) with the realities of the modern, scientific world no longer place credibility in myths that are patently untrue in either a real or imagined sense. Such stories can have merit only in the minds of grossly ignorant people. Clearly, the message from those who employ higher order thinking skills is: "Get up to speed in the 21st century, or get left behind."

~~~~~~~~~~~~~~~~~~

Fossils and religious dogma have this in common: they are both frozen in time and are incapable of evolving in a rapidly changing world. Extinction comes to mind.

~~~~~~~~~~~~~~~~~~

The greatest abuse and misuse of power is found in religious faith.

~~~~~~~~~~~~~~~~~~

Anyone who teaches that this life on earth is but a proving ground to determine if people spend eternity after death in a kind of paradise, or in a state of eternal pain and torment is preaching a philosophy of death, not a philosophy for living.

~~~~~~~~~~~~~~~~~~

When religionists argue that their religion is true and others are false, what they are arguing is that their religious myth is superior to all other religious myths. This is the height of absurdity. All myths are the product of human imagination and wishful thinking. No myth has any claim to objective reality, and for many, none is claimed.

~~~~~~~~~~~~~~~~~~

Faith is belief in unsubstantiated, unconfirmed, unverified ideas, or as Paul of Tarsus wrote: "things hoped for, but unseen." If this is so, then of what value can new knowledge and critical thinking be if people can arrive at the truth in such a manner? The people responsible for building new and great civilizations were visionary, innovative, creative liberals who introduced profound changes. The people responsible for the decay and inevitable collapse of those civilizations were conservatives who favored the status quo and loved to say, "God is in his heaven, all is right with the world."

~~~~~~~~~~~~~~~~~~

The non acceptance of others and the intolerance of their ideas grows with the strength and certainty of one's religious faith. Bigotry nearly always grows from religious faith—ungrounded absolutist thinking.

~~~~~~~~~~~~~~~~~~~~

The Crucifix is a barbaric icon of ignorance and perversion.

~~~~~~~~~~~~~~~~~~~~

Faith is the mother of hatred whenever people identify their moral imperatives in religious terms.

~~~~~~~~~~~~~~~~~~~~

Evil people find refuge in overt piety. Consider George W. Bush's never-ending references to his god.

~~~~~~~~~~~~~~~~~~~~

With unjustified certitude, anything is possible.

~~~~~~~~~~~~~~~~~~~~

Prayer is just another form of mental masturbation. It may feel good, but it is pure fantasy, and a poor substitute for the real thing.

~~~~~~~~~~~~~~~~~~~~

Religions arrive at their "truths" that Mother Nature and her laws of the universe neither endorse nor defend.

~~~~~~~~~~~~~~~~~~~~

Religious beliefs are faith based and fact free.

~~~~~~~~~~~~~~~~~~~~

Religious believers are deafened by their faith and blinded by their ideology.

~~~~~~~~~~~~~~~~~

We should ask ourselves, "How much joyful laughter have the world's religions given us?

~~~~~~~~~~~~~~~~~

Since a personal savior and creator god is the product of fear, ignorance, and barbaric superstition, the continued existence of such a god is dependent on the perpetuation of fear, ignorance, and superstition. Such is the role of the priests and their functional analogs.

~~~~~~~~~~~~~~~~~

Unhesitating certainty (faith) is the behavior of foolish and ignorant people. Intelligent, educated people practice restraint and reflective thinking before giving tentative and provisional assent to the claims and assertions of others, otherwise they would be credulous fools and deservedly so.

~~~~~~~~~~~~~~~~~

If you have religious faith you never have to do your home work, indeed there is no homework.

~~~~~~~~~~~~~~~~~

Since the "soul" is the essence of consciousness, and consciousness is the function of a viable brain, does it not follow that the "soul" becomes an indefensible idea when the brain dies?

~~~~~~~~~~~~~~~~~~~~~

Is the religious dogmatic assertion of the creation of the universe ex nihilo by a deity more intelligible or instructive than the "Big Bang" theory advanced by modern scientific cosmologists?

~~~~~~~~~~~~~~~~~~~~~

Religious faith is the will and the way to avoid learning the truth about natural phenomena.

~~~~~~~~~~~~~~~~~~~~~

It is extremely doubtful that there is any group of people in the world who collectively are as scientifically illiterate about natural phenomena as are the clergy. However, this does not deter them for one minute from making the most egregious errors and the most dogmatic statements with all the sincerity and passion at their command about these same natural phenomena.

~~~~~~~~~~~~~~~~~~~~~

Theology is institutionalized and sanctified ignorance and superstition perpetuated and promulgated by the ignorant and the superstitious. Is it then worthy of our attention?

~~~~~~~~~~~~~~~~~~~~~

No field of intellectual endeavor is as riddled with as much egregious error as theology. Produced and promulgated in the complete absence of any science or objectivity of any kind, theology has been, and still is, a kind of intellectual masturbation that has infected and retarded the growth and development of Western Civilization for over 3000 years.

~~~~~~~~~~~~~~~~~~~~~

By giving assent to the irrational absurdities of organized religions, we invite unmitigated societal disasters.

~~~~~~~~~~~~~~~~~~

In a world that burgeons with chaos, superstition, fear, ambiguity, uncertainty and ignorance, there are two kinds of people: those who seek to understand through critical thinking, science and rationality (higher intellectual function) and those who try to cope with the illusions of faith, denial and the irrationality of revealed religion.

~~~~~~~~~~~~~~~~~~

When we were children in school, we learned about the ancient religious mythologies of the Greeks, the Romans, the Babylonians, the Persians, the Egyptians and others. The myths were taught as such, and we understood them as such. They were not taught as factual history, nor with historical characters. Now, why is it that so many people believe that the ancient Hebrew religious myths were about historical events with historical people? There can be no other explanation than the fact that the Roman Catholic church, and its Protestant derivatives, insisted that these myths be taught as factual history. This is classic fraud and academic dishonesty. Shame on the perpetrators and promulgators of this intellectual crime. Lying to our impressionable, trusting children is the most heinous kind of child abuse.

~~~~~~~~~~~~~~~~~~

Religions are founded by radical, idealistic mystics who eventually ossify into absolutist institutions dominated by authoritarian literalists who declare all independent creative thinking as heresy and blasphemy. It is the same old game of power and control by megalomaniacs whose appetite for power and dominion over others knows no boundaries.

~~~~~~~~~~~~~~~~~~~

A myth is a story created by imaginative people to explain what they don't adequately understand—the inexplicable. This is why all religions are grounded in a gross misunderstanding and misinterpretation of natural phenomena.

~~~~~~~~~~~~~~~~~~~

Religious faith exempts and shields the believers from the intellectual errors of the past. Science rigorously searches and exposes its own errors.

~~~~~~~~~~~~~~~~~~~

The subjective intuitive means of explaining natural phenomena derived from ancient religious texts has turned out to be an epistemological and cultural disaster of error after error. The scientific, objective, quantitative approach to explaining natural phenomena, while frequently counterintuitive, has provided us with reliable, verifiable knowledge that has made it possible to manage our lives in a rewarding, productive manner. This comparison is worth our attention.

~~~~~~~~~~~~~~~~~~~

The objective of a teacher is to enable the student to transcend the teacher and become independent of him/her. The objective of the priest is to capture and control the minds of the "sheeple" in their flock and make them dependent, subservient and obedient. It is the oldest and most enduring con game in the world. The derivatives of the mystical, mythological monotheistic religions are: absolutism, authoritarianism, totalitarianism, magical thinking, divisiveness, intolerance, bigotry, persecution and violence. We should rethink our allegiance to such a destructive and unrewarding kind of world view.

~~~~~~~~~~~~~~~~~

Religious faith enables one to live a lie with impunity.

~~~~~~~~~~~~~~~~~

People have told me that I should respect the religious views of others even if they are in contradiction to my understanding of what is intellectually defensible. This is absurd. I am under no obligation whatsoever to respect the views of others that I have reason to believe are contradictory to reason, logic and the known laws of the universe.

~~~~~~~~~~~~~~~~~

Either truth or comfort is one's highest priority. We need to choose.

~~~~~~~~~~~~~~~~~

Religious "truths" are intrinsically dangerous because they lack the objectivity necessary for evaluation in the bright light of reality.

~~~~~~~~~~~~~~~~~

The most resistance to discussion of religion and politics comes from those who believe they already possess the truth.

~~~~~~~~~~~~~~~~~

Has there ever been a religion that placed the development of the human mind as its highest priority?

~~~~~~~~~~~~~~~~~

Human misery is a profoundly sad spectacle that is greatly exacerbated when cloaked in moral righteousness.

~~~~~~~~~~~~~~~~~~

Since academic honesty and intellectual integrity are of prime importance to us, being an atheist is an ethical imperative and a moral obligation.

~~~~~~~~~~~~~~~~~~

The primary fault of faith is that it doesn't have any verifiable cognitive support.

~~~~~~~~~~~~~~~~~~

Religious faith is how ignorant people employ superstition to cope with uncertainty.

~~~~~~~~~~~~~~~~~~

Intelligent, educated adults divest themselves of the biases, prejudices, irrationalities and superstitions they acquired in their childhood. Children cling to these intellectual traps their entire life.

~~~~~~~~~~~~~~~~~~

The promise of heaven for those who fervently believe the absurdities and irrationalities of Christian dogma is an epistemological Ponzi scheme.

~~~~~~~~~~~~~~~~~~

An atheist is a person who recognizes and acknowledges the lies of religion and refuses to give them serious consideration.

~~~~~~~~~~~~~~~~~~

Religious faith is a license people hold up to shield themselves from logic, reason and critical thinking when evidence is lacking to support irrational religious doctrine.

~~~~~~~~~~~~~~~~~~

Subjective certitudes, like religious faith, can sanction any kind of fanaticism or atrocity.

~~~~~~~~~~~~~~~~~~

True spirituality neither requires nor allows a consideration of a deity.

~~~~~~~~~~~~~~~~~~

There are people with varying degrees of expertise in the scientific community, but there are no authority figures. Authority figures would soon produce doctrine and dogma which are antithetical to science. The tentative and provisional nature of scientific truths rules out authority figures.

About the Author

Even as a child I think I was probably a natural skeptic. My Mother told me in my early adulthood that even as a preschooler when I was covered with the baloney (a nice word for bullshit) that some adults are prone to dropping on small children, that I would respond with my squinty-eyed look and blurt out "I don't believe it!" Skepticism was a good thing then, and it is a good thing now.

My Mother saw to it that I was indoctrinated in the the Presbyterian church as a child, and was confirmed as a member of the faith as an adolescent. I don't think that she did this out of devotion to the church or out of religious zeal. I think that she did this because she thought she was supposed to do so—something like an expectation of the culture in which we lived. My Father must have just followed my Mother's lead on the matter because I do not recall him ever saying a single word either in favor of or against, religious ideas. He invariably fell asleep during Sunday morning services, especially during the sermons. Later I understood why. Sermons are rarely intellectually stimulating or challenging. More often brain-numbing boredom comes to mind.

By the time I entered High School I was a Christian by default. Like my peers, I had not been exposed to any other credo, especially any other competing or contrasting ideas. I had become a passive victim of unintended intellectual child abuse by well intentioned parents.

I asked so many pointed and probing questions during my indoctrination that I think our pastor must have thought I was some kind of pest. Sometimes his eyes would roll when I asked a question. After all—I was supposed to blindly accept as truth what I was told was the truth. I was supposed to believe the received word of God—not question it. I don't recall ever getting any satisfying answers to my questions—more often than not I was put off when the pastor would say, "We'll take that up later." It seems as though I always had a hard time accepting the propaganda of any kind of authority figure. Thus, the answers I got for my questions always left a great deal to be desired, probably because they did not have the ring of truth to my skeptical ears.

I joined the Navy on July 12th, 1948, with a few of my friends and spent my enlistment as an aviation electronics technician. When my three year enlistment was over, (plus an additional year at the pleasure of The President) I returned to my home town in N.W. Wisconsin. I was still a Christian because I had not been exposed to any competing ideology. I was still at the default stage of my religious experience. I knew that I had four years of college education available on the G.I. Bill if I kept my nose clean and performed adequately. I wasn't going to let that get away.

In September in 1952 I matriculated at the Wisconsin State College at Eau Claire, if for no other reason than it was the closest and least expensive four year college. The next four years were the most formative years of my life, as I am sure it was for anyone. While I satisfied the requirements for two science majors and the other curricular requirements of a B.S., I was also certified to be a science teacher which was my career choice as a teenager. I was in daily contact with many highly educated and sophisticated people whose life style was a sharp contrast to the minds with whom I was forced to associate in the Navy. Much of the education pursuing a college degree is by design, but much of it is by osmosis from the people with whom one associates.

I learned about the scientific method of seeking truth about the physical and the factual, about critical thinking skills, and about the need for evidentiary support for one's assertions or claims. My natural skepticism fit very well with my science education. I learned about the Arts in Humanities, about Political Science, Sociology and History. I learned about Logic and Philosophy. The scales of religious obscurantism that had built up over years of the muddled-headed thinking and the subjective speculation of theology had begun to fall away from my eyes. The ecclesiastical fog bank of Christianity faded away and my vision of reality cleared. I could now see the world as it was instead of the preordained religious view of some ancient, ideological zealot.

Christianity—indeed the Abrahamic religions—now faded into oblivion in my mind as a viable world view. I was now living in the real world of educated adults instead of a childlike fantasy world of the monotheistic religions. I was an apostate before I finished my sophomore year in college. It was an intellectual awakening. The fear, guilt, shame, sin and death that occupies the mind of nearly all Christians was purged from my mind. Life now was a kind of modern, joyful exuberance unencumbered by ancient, archaic ideas of what the world and my life were about. I now defined "God" as "The nature of Nature." Biblical miracles and fantastical tales concocted from the minds of ignorant priests from an alien zeitgeist that flew in the face of the known laws of the universe had been expunged from my mind. I was now finally on the road to living free of the superstition and magical thinking of the religious indoctrination that had corrupted my mind for more than twenty years.

In 1962, after the first six years of my career, I was fortunate to receive a National Science Foundation Academic Year Scholarship at the University of Utah. At the conclusion of my study there I received a Masters degree in Science Education in 1963. This made a huge contribution to my professional growth and competence as a teacher of biology and chemistry. It also confirmed and expanded my secular world view.

Many of the Christians I know (some of whom are ordained Christian ministers) struggle mightily with the internal conflict and cognitive dissonance that is immanent with the profound intellectual contradictions in their religion. For some it is emotionally very traumatic. I am sure that they would like to divest themselves of this baggage, but the indelible indoctrination they received as children, and the subsequent experience of being immersed in the religious myth for so long, has made it nearly impossible for them to jettison this virus of the mind. They are literally trapped in an intellectual and emotional black hole from which there is no escape for them. For those who were able to come to grips with the absurdities of the

Biblical/religious world view and admit to themselves that they had been conned and tragically wrong for so long—that they had been living a lie—that they had been part and parcel to promulgating and propagating falsehoods, I can only applaud them and offer my support as they transform themselves into a higher plane of existence as human beings who are free of the insidious intellectual malignancy of the revealed religions.

Gloria Steinem once opined that religion was "just politics made sacred." I whole heartedly agree. Whether politics or religion, it is still a game of power and control. Kings used the sword to force compliance with their dictates, but the priest/bishop messed with people's minds. Between the two of them they wielded deadly effective weapons on the ignorant masses. When the state gets in bed with the church, tyranny and oppression soon follow. These two totalitarian regimes in concert with each other have historically been very hard to beat. Then, in the eighteenth century, in some English colonies in North America, the Founding Fathers of America rebelled under the yoke of authoritarian tyranny and explicitly rejected the totalitarian regimes of the Crown and the Church. They divested themselves of the tyranny that had been oppressing them when they crafted a new secular nation whose constitution began, "We the people . . . ."

Free from the totalitarian regimes of the State and the Church, America has prospered like no other nation under a new secular paradigm.

I now have a growing list of people I know who have impressive academic credentials in theology who have mustered the courage to admit to themselves and others that theology and the Christian scheme of things are fraught through and through with intellectually untenable and indefensible absurdities that they could not, in good conscience, maintain the masquerade any longer. They had to pull the plug on the charade they had been perpetuating and promulgating to salvage whatever academic honesty and intellectual integrity they had remaining. It must have been gut-grinding experience for them to admit that they had been conned into believing to be true what so many had recognized as a bogus world view from the beginning.

Walking on water, an intelligible voice coming from a burning bush and other alleged "miracles" that defy and deny the known laws of the universe are ideas still being endorsed by most Christians. This is literalism at its worst and the root of the fundamentalism that has corrupted the minds of so many believers. This is both an intellectual and cultural travesty because people act on their beliefs. When people's beliefs are not only irrational and illogical, their actions are frequently irrational and illogical. The implementation of policies that are grounded in and derived from illogical and irrational ideas result in the despoliation of our planet, unmitigated suffering, and unnecessary bloodshed and death. Religious thinking will have to be abandoned if we are to avoid extinction in the near future. The problems the world has cannot be satisfactorily solved in time to prevent our mutual self destruction unless the religious paradigm is abandoned.

In spite of the fact that my views as expressed herein are held firmly, I live comfortably with the reality that I am a fallible and imperfect human being.

I have made errors in the past and will undoubtedly make more in the future. This does not, however, take away from my convictions which, I hope, are always grounded in solid evidence and are confirmable. I freely submit to rigorous examination of my ideas and, consistent with good science, regard all truths to be tentative, provisional, incomplete and imperfect.

Now, after a thirty-five year career as a high school biology and chemistry teacher, and nineteen years of retirement, I am turning eighty-one years of age in the spring of 2010. I'm looking forward to at least twenty more years of intellectual and emotional freedom from the debilitating and suffocating effects of religious superstition, irrationality and magical thinking.

When my tenure as a member of the Earth's natural biota ends, the only place I will be "going" is back to the Earth, like every other living thing on this planet. It is good.

I am still vertical, mobile and smiling.

All this without any God Talk and Other Incoherent Religious Delusions.

LaVergne, TN USA
18 May 2010
183144LV00003B/7/P